WITHDRAWN

MOMADAY, VIZENOR, ARMSTRONG

AMERICAN INDIAN LITERATURE AND CRITICAL STUDIES SERIES
GERALD VIZENOR AND LOUIS OWENS, GENERAL EDITORS

Also by Hartwig Isernhagen

(ed.) *The U.S. from Within: A Workbook for Students* (Munich, 1976)
Ästhetische Innovation and Kulturkritik: Das Frühwerk von John Dos Passos, 1916–1938 (Munich, 1983)
Interdisziplinarität und die gesellschaftliche Rolle der Geistes- und Kulturwissenschaften heute (Basel, 1997)

Momaday, Vizenor, Armstrong

CONVERSATIONS ON
AMERICAN INDIAN WRITING

HARTWIG ISERNHAGEN

University of Oklahoma Press : Norman

Published with the assistance of the National Endowment for the Humanities, a federal agency which supports the study of such fields as history, philosophy, literature, and language.

Library of Congress Cataloging-in-Publication Data

Isernhagen, Hartwig, 1940–
    Momaday, Vizenor, Armstrong : conversations on American Indian
    writing / Hartwig Isernhagen.
        p.   cm. — (American Indian literature and critical studies
    series ; v. 32)
      ISBN 0-8061-3120-9 (alk. paper)
        1. American literature—Indian authors—History and criticism—
    Theory, etc.   2. Canadian literature—Indian authors—History and
    criticism—Theory, etc.   3. Authors, American—20th century—
    Interviews.   4. Authors, Canadian—20th century—Interviews.
    5. Indian authors—North America—Interviews.   6. Momaday, N. Scott,
    1934–   —Interviews.   7. Vizenor, Gerald Robert, 1934–
    —Interviews.   8. Armstrong, Jeannette C.—Interviews.   9. Indians of
    North America—Interviews.   10. Indians in literature.   I. Title.
    II. Series.
    PS153.I52I84   1999
    810.9'897—dc21   98-40682
                                                                          CIP

Momaday, Vizenor, Armstrong: Conversations on American Indian Writing is Volume 32 in the American Indian Literature and Critical Studies Series.

The paper in this book meets the guidelines for permanence and durability of the Committee on Production Guidelines for Book Longevity of the Council on Library Resources, Inc. ∞

1 2 3 4 5 6 7 8 9 10

This book is dedicated to all who were with me on journeys through those physical and mental landscapes that are subsumed under the name "Indian country." It is dedicated, above all, to a child playing in Canyon de Chelly and to two adults looking on.

Contents

Acknowledgments ix

Introduction: Prejudices, Aims, and Procedures 3

The Questions 21

Interviews

    N. Scott Momaday 29

    Gerald Vizenor 77

    Jeannette Armstrong 135

Acknowledgments

I am indebted, most obviously and most indelibly, to the three authors with whom I had these conversations. Beyond that, I owe thanks to Marianne Aversa, who transcribed the text from tapes that were far from perfect technically, and to students at Basel and Berne who helped me develop a fuller sense of what I was (and am) trying to do. Kim Wiar's energetic efforts on behalf of the manuscript and Sarah Iselin's patient copyediting will be remembered with gratitude. Through the Association for Canadian Studies in German-Speaking Countries and the International Council for Canadian Studies, the Canadian government provided several travel grants that allowed me to familiarize myself with the contemporary cultural production of First Nations people in Canada, and I am grateful for this support. It is impossible to specify the more general debt I owe to colleagues and professional organizations that during the last fifteen years offered me innumerable opportunities to air my views and gave me invaluable feedback; but this debt is intensely felt.

HARTWIG ISERNHAGEN

Basel, July, 1998

MOMADAY, VIZENOR, ARMSTRONG

INTRODUCTION

Prejudices, Aims, and Procedures

These interviews were taped during the summer of 1994. I talked to N. Scott Momaday on July 20, in my room at the La Fonda hotel in Santa Fe; to Gerald Vizenor on July 26, in his office at the University of California, Berkeley: and to Jeannette Armstrong on August 10, at the En'owkin Centre in Penticton, British Columbia. Apart from minor interruptions for cassette changes or incoming telephone calls, the interviews were done in one sitting, ranging freely over one and the same series of questions, which were communicated to the three authors in advance. I hoped the conversations would thus form a triad held together by a single horizon of understanding and concern, at the same time that they developed with sufficient spontaneity to mirror the considerable differences among the three authors in terms of oeuvre and personality: if their modes of writing are different, so are the designs that have shaped their lives. In sum, the interviews were intended to establish, for interviewer and interviewee, both a shared pattern of interests and some space for the play of differences. My concern for spontaneity was always dominant. The questions, for example, were regarded as entirely functional: if they elicited something interesting, it did not usually matter to me if they had been taken in exactly the way in which I had meant them.

In putting together the questionnaire—which the methodical, or methodologically inclined, reader will find following this introduction—I was considerably aided, directly and indirectly, by a seminar on American Indian literature that I taught as a guest at the University of Berne during the spring semester of 1994. One set of questions refers to such general problems as the viability of notions of Nativeness in criticism, the relation between literatures and audiences, the cultural legitimation of creative and critical writing, as well as the internationalization of notions of the indigene, in part through the establishment of international networks of Native writers and organizations. Other questions address writerly strategies and, especially, the ability to counter stereotyping, to establish better images of self and other—which poses the question what a "better" image is—and to represent and accommodate the changes of history. In the same area lay the vast subject how one can avoid writing from within a conception of cultural and literary history that is shaped by the views and values of the majority and will thus be oppressive to minorities. In this context, too, arose questions regarding the relevance of standard critical terms (and of the academy in general) to Native writing today, at the same time that notions of poly-traditionality, poly-vocality, and interculturality became more and more deeply embedded in the discourses of interviewees and interviewer. Finally, questions regarding the formation of cultural-political alliances (largely under the heading of the minoritarian) pointed in the direction of social action, as did the specific topic of the representation or thematization of violence in the texts of the three authors and American Indian writing in general.

This volume is different from other, similar enterprises in bringing together only three authors. Thereby, it did not impose on the interviewer the burden of having to accommodate a great variety of viewpoints, which might have forced him into a more or less neutral or chameleonlike attitude. Initially, I did hover uneasily between two roles: that of the interviewer proper, which is entirely a subservient one, intent on eliciting more or less specific information from the interviewee; and that of an equal partner in a conversation or discussion, in a shared act of inquiry. Recognizing how obviously the questions reflected my own understanding of and interests in American Indian literature, I have from quite early on in the process consciously given preference to the equal partner role. I have occasionally moved into the foreground to introduce different viewpoints that appeared relevant, to open up habitualized responses by the frequently interviewed authors, and quite simply to get my own voice into the text. I have accepted certain risks, and I view each of these exchanges as an invitation to the reader to join the two interlocutors in a process of reflection and a search for what may, if we are lucky, interest all three of us. Finally, if the interviewer again and again becomes a partner in this dialogue, rather than a figure of mediation between the author and his (or her) readers, this has also to be seen in the context of current debates about the possibility of an independently European perspective in North American studies.

Specifically, I have felt free to insert my own views on the problems of legitimation encountered by contemporary Native writing (not only in North America). And I have felt free to foreground a question that was already implied in my decision whom I would ask for these interviews: the question of the use of terms describing periods or movements. Jeannette Armstrong would probably be labeled a realist by most critics (at least for her fiction); N. Scott Momaday, a modernist; and Gerald Vizenor, a postmodernist. Such labeling is obviously useful as a first approach, but it can become a positive hindrance to understanding if it is misconceived as reflecting a simple historical sequence. We do, of course, have realism, modernism, and postmodernism as period concepts, but in the present context the terms acquire a different usage—one that will, incidentally, also emerge from any close look at the period concepts themselves. The discussion of postmodernism is shot through with references to the impossibility of cleanly separating postmodernist and modernist strategies of writing, as well as to the constant reemergence of realisms in both contexts; and modernism is so pervasively defined in terms of recoveries of deeper realities that it cannot be separated from the internally very conflicted discussion of the historical forms of realism. This highly fruitful terminological and conceptual muddle indicates, on the one hand, that a historical "style" is created as a momentarily dominant combination of transhistorically available possibilities of writing, while, on the other hand, even such notions of dominance cannot be taken to solve the historian's problem out of hand.

The labels "realistic," "modernist," and "postmodernist" are hence not to be taken to imply a historical sequencing of the discourses of the three authors: it is much more useful to see the three as sharing a historical moment of great complexity. By pointing out salient characteristics, the labels serve as an approach to the interviews—in which they are, gratifyingly enough, more or less instantly and quite organically deconstructed to a considerable degree. Momaday's insistence on the dignity of the single word, his search for valid symbols of existence, his grounding of the authority of the writer in the creative power of language—all of these characteristics exist within the context of modernist attempts to create a literature that will be a "momentary stay against confusion." At the same time, Momaday has localized the universal discourse of modernism. Ever since his seminal "Man Made of Words" speech,[1] he has resolutely applied that international idiom in the service of the survival of Native discourses, giving them greater cultural visibility and prestige, and he has made modernism deal with specific, urgent questions of material and political life. In this context he has often had to resort to an almost postmodern gesture of deconstructing established stereotypes and debilitating points of view.

Vizenor's work can be read as the appropriation of the equally international idiom of postmodernism for similar purposes, although along different lines. His distrust of the instant commodification of language, and of the destructive power and inescapability of stereotype, is akin to standard postmodernist/ deconstructionist positions; and so is his solution, which is to ground the authority of the writer in processes (rather than products) of utterance. His texts slip from one statement, term, or symbol to another. Nothing is fixed except for a will-to-survival that is equally as strong as Momaday's. And so, ever since his days in journalism, Vizenor has also fixed his focus on the material exigencies of life, which infuses a degree of realism into his work.

Momaday and Vizenor have emerged as individual artists from backgrounds already characterized by a successful negotiation of the space between Native and non-Native cultures. The same is true of Jeannette Armstrong, with a figure like Mourning Dove[2] among her ancestors, but she has much more program-

1. N. Scott Momaday, "The Man Made of Words," in *Indian Voices: The First Convocation of American Indian Scholars* (San Francisco: Indian Historian Press, n. d. [c. 1970]), 49–62.
2. Mourning Dove, or Hum-ishu-ma, was the author (with the collaboration of L. C. McWhorter) of *Cogewea: The Half-Blood* (1927) and *Coyote Stories* (1933).

matically established herself, or constructed her artistic persona, in terms of multiple relations with a specific Native community, her fellow Okanagans in and near Penticton. The urgency of political questions confronting her community has made her rely on and adapt forms of referential discourse that tend to be called realistic. As I have said, the highly diverse ways in which new literatures everywhere revalidate these literary forms should make short shrift of linear histories that attempt to relegate realism to the past through such labelling. While this aspect of Jeannette Armstrong's oeuvre may in part have been shaped by her manifold teaching and organizational duties—connected, above all, with the En'owkin Centre and its School of Writing—another aspect of her writings (and her life) has been deeply affected by her intimate contact with Harry Robinson, the great traditional Okanagan storyteller. Notions of translation (from Native languages into English, from oral into written form, from communal experience into individually produced texts) have therefore necessarily been prominent in her approach to the teaching and the practice of writing. At the same time, her involvement with Theytus Books—to my knowledge the only entirely Native-owned publishing house in North America—must have extended the scope of her concern with the role of writing in identity politics, from community to nation.

Thus the three authors represent three ways of writing as well as three patterns of cultural survival. They also stand for three different ways of balancing writing and teaching. Scott Momaday's oeuvre is most clearly to be found in individual volumes marked with his name. Jeannette Armstrong's production very much also includes writers whom she directly or indirectly has "made." Gerald Vizenor's work occupies the ground between writing and teaching, and between "the creative" and "the critical," in very original ways that appear to be designed to abolish the very borderline between those categories. Taken as a group—however haphazardly brought together by the interviewing process—they should probably be seen as makers of literature and of other cultural products and events, rather than as writers pure and simple. In this broad perspective, I hope the volume as a whole displays the extent of the differences among Native North American writers, while at the same time, it does not give in to the twin temptations of (impossible) completeness (which would only have led to a fragmented picture) and simplistic systematization. In representing realistic, modernist, and postmodernist tendencies in current Native writing, these interviews suggest the continued vitality of those movements and the possibility of multiple inter-actions among them.

The attempt to draw the reader into a conversation deter-mines the shape of the volume. The interviews engaged the three authors in an exchange of ideas that displays their perspectives on writing and society; they show the authors in dialogues that explore implications and ramifications of their positions. I do not try to provide the type of specific information on background and development, or the statements of opinion, that are a prominent object of standard interviews—and that make them so similar to one another. (A lot of such material is available in important publications on Momaday and Vizenor, and on Armstrong in only slightly more out-of-the-way media.) There is no index that would enable one to find X's opinion on this or that at one glance. I do not intend that readers will go and check quickly, for example, what Momaday has to say about *House Made of Dawn*, though a little patient reading may show that several things he says—with and without explicit reference to that book—do impinge on its interpretation. These interviews make a contribution largely in the shape and mode of the interaction between the participants, or in the way in which information unfolds in argument and other forms of discourse, rather than in terms of fact. How far they succeed, is for the reader to say.

My goal of drawing in the reader accounts, too, for the relative length of the individual exchanges: opinions and judgments are often concisely stated, but just as frequently they will emerge from the conversation in ways that are part of the message because they contextualize it. To isolate statements would be to rob the texts of much or most of their impact. This is also why these interviews are comparatively close to the transcripts; they are intended to invite further work by having a degree of openness about them, rather than aiming at any type of closure. I hope they will nonetheless give the reader a degree of pleasure in the act of reading; my aim was a fusion of intellectual rigor and jouissance.

Going over the transcripts of the original interviews, I felt a
desire to return to the authors with questions or suggestions.
These supplementary questions and comments appear in foot-
notes at the points where they occurred to me in reading the
interviews. I invited the authors to answer or make suggestions in
their turn, and to insert questions of their own. Jeannette Armstrong and Gerald Vizenor made use of this opportunity more
extensively than Scott Momaday did, which is entirely in keeping
with the slightly different function my comments had in the three
exchanges. My comments to Momaday were largely intended to
throw added light on his very finished utterances, which aimed at
a high degree of closure, and that is why they took the form of
comments rather than questions. In the other two interviews my
additions attempt to carry forward the innate momentum of the
conversations. The whole enterprise thus continued into 1995 and
1997, and the final form of the interviews, as printed here, is
intended to preserve some of their open-endedness. The texts also
preserve their original conversational qualities and the occasional
power plays (always good-natured, I thought) between the interviewer and the interviewee. It is not for me to judge whether the
interviews also give some inkling of the extraordinary intensity
that many moments in these exchanges had for myself—à propos of
something else, Jeannette Armstrong has the apt phrase "moments
of unique interaction" in her interview. Yet, in rereading the texts, I
cannot but hear the three voices that produced them.

The shapes of the three texts were ultimately determined by
the original set of questions and the actual interviews meandering
(and jumping) through a field of interrelated topics. I did not try
to impose any simple linear sequence on them. Similar questions
therefore recur at different points and in different contexts, and
there are breaks in the flow of the conversations as I go back to my
prepared questions. I have not tried to abolish these traits, because
between the recurrences and across the breaks an internal dialogue seems to me to come into being within each text: a sort of
intratextual intertextuality that mirrors our minds' dependence on
the particular configurations of the moment. In order to produce
three texts of roughly similar outer appearance, however, the
manuscripts had to be tidied up in somewhat different ways. Both

N. Scott Momaday and Gerald Vizenor chose to conduct the interviews in a highly professional and often magisterial manner, producing some utterances that were very formal, though in the main still of a conversational kind. Their texts have only been cleansed of the occasional fillers and repetitions that are unavoidable in spontaneous exchanges. I have been careful to preserve those indications of hesitation or revisions of phrasing that appeared to offer some insight into the workings of the author's mind or the particular moment in the interview process. The criterion was in effect the readability of the particular deviation from a "perfect" (written) text.

Jeannette Armstrong, on the other hand, chose to speak quite informally, which may in part be because (for some reason unknown to me) I inquired much more directly about her own practices than I did with the other two authors. (Upon reflection, I believe this may in part be due to my interest in the En'owkin School of Writing; questions relating to it would necessarily elicit her own administrative, critical, and creative views.) The interview with Armstrong contained many more of those breaks in syntax and apparent loops in the line of argument that are the hallmark of a very informal conversation rather than the semiformal interview. Wherever these traits violated the decorum of the written text (as they sometimes unfortunately will), so as to hamper its proper reception, it had to be normalized. I hope I have done so with enough tact and skill not to interfere with the essentially conversational qualities of the text, which to me are part of its particular value, or with Jeannette Armstrong's characteristic voice. My own questions and comments have been rephrased to get rid of some of the infelicities a nonnative speaker will unavoidably produce under stress, and they have been pruned where necessary.

Whatever my own role in determining the final shape of the texts, they were approved for publication in this form by the three authors. And they appear here in the sequence in which the interviews were conducted, since I can see that in some places they build on one another. They may do so in other ways that I do not recognize, which is further reason to document the interviews and the editing process. In this ultimately quite open form, the book is addressed to a multiple audience: above all, to attentive and enthusiastic readers of Native literature, both inside the academy and (I hope) outside it, though general readers may occasionally need to exercise a little patience with isolated moments of high academicism in the texts; and to undergraduate and graduate students as well as teachers of literature, and thus to colleagues of the interviewer—but those should be among the enthusiastic readers anyway. The disciplinary context would comprise not only Native North American literature, but also the other emergent literatures in English, English and American literature in general, and comparative literature. Such a variety of readers will read both the interviews and this introduction differently. In a highly conflicted field like American Indian`literature, some degree of misreading will probably be unavoidable, and much more real disagreement may be expected. If it plays itself out in the spirit of underlying cooperation that characterizes the interviews, I will be quite satisfied.

Beyond the foregoing comments on differences among the authors that influenced the interviews, I will not characterize, comment on, or interpret these texts. They need to stand or fall by themselves. But I do wish to fill out the sketch that I have already begun of what I thought I was doing in conducting them, and how I did it, and why.

I have used the phrase "an invitation to join in a process" to characterize this volume. In the interviews I aimed for a type of dialogue that has for some time been axiomatic and normative in such enterprises, and far beyond them, in all exchanges among ethnocultural groups and across other lines of difference. The normative status of dialogicity only raises the much more difficult and complex question what precisely constitutes a good dialogue, and, shifting shapes, the interviews may open up spaces within which possibilities for good dialogues will develop. My purpose was not predominantly an act of positioning, not to determine a point on which one may build, but rather to clear a field in which one may move.

Yet, to move in that space does imply a general historical and political position insofar as in it a colonial/postcolonial history is opened up for discussion—certainly not for the first time, but

probably not for the last time either—a history that America and
the world have tried to close. Alan Trachtenberg's discourse, in
The Incorporation of America: Culture and Society in the Gilded Age, is
sufficiently removed from the pieties of our moment to be
enlightening when he points out that

> history seemed for [Teddy] Roosevelt, for Turner, for
> countless others contemplating the westward experience,
> a foreclosed event, an inevitable advance from low to
> high, from simple to complex, and in more senses than
> one, from "Indian" to "American.". . . In this "progress,"
> this proof of "America," the profoundest role was
> reserved not for the abundance of land but for the fatal
> presence of the Indian. . . . "Civilization" required a
> "savagery" against which to distinguish itself.[3]

Attempts to break open that closure and foreclosure are currently
de rigueur, and the notion of progress itself that was used to
"savage" the Indian has more recently been associated with a
potentially liberating imagery of cultural hybridity. In multicultural postmodernity, there should be space for good dialogues,
and perhaps there is more than there used to be; but I have used
the phrase "the pieties of our moment" just now because it seems
there is not enough space, and the dialogues too frequently are not
good enough. The very notion of multicultural postmodernity, as
a translation of the notion of progress or a definition of its latest
(last?) stage, has become just as prescriptive as any earlier view of
any civilized present, and if (to quote Trachtenberg again) "official
national policy stopped short of extermination; it settled for
abolishing Native ways of life and their obstructive practices" (28),
one may well ask whether the current climate may not work in the
same direction. In the past,

> the Turner thesis, which defines the land as "free" and
> identifies Indians with "wilderness," as a "common dan-
> ger," . . . [served as a] veil: it fails to see Indians as other

3. Alan Trachtenberg, *The Incorporation of America: Culture and Society in the
Gilded Age* (New York: Hill and Wang, 1982), 26–27.

than undifferentiated "savages" in the path of "social evolution" from "frontier" to "city and factory system." To see
Indians as "savage" is already to define them out of existence, to define them only in relation to their apparent
opposite: "civilized" society. (28–29)

May not our present norm of hybridity become another such veil,
through which we will see American Indians as just as (ir)rele-
vantly different as any other ethnic group, and just as much on the
path of social evolution from monoculturalism to multiculturalism
as anyone else? The postmodern iconography of history, of its
process and its ultimate products, may be just as much shaped by
the preemptive perspectives of the dominant majority as the
iconography of enlightened and emancipatory Western civilization was when it so frighteningly turned into its own opposite in
nineteenth-century dealings with Indians.

What is lacking, perhaps, is a fruitful skepticism of all ideo-
logies, or something like that gesture of questioning that will be
discussed later as a source of writerly authority. Here, the dialogue intended in these interviews may emblematize a possible
alliance between certain makers of Native literature and some
among the purveyors of a liberal (or liberal arts) education. Such
an alliance might be grounded in similar views of what education
is, and in similarities vis-à-vis society at large. After an earlier
exchange with Jeannette Armstrong about Harry Robinson, I
could not help wondering whether what she had talked about as
his aims in the creation of meaning—giving preference to implication (rather than information), to the work as a source of varied
meanings (rather than its momentary reception in terms of this or
that message), to personal growth as a series of stages of perception (rather than the accumulation of knowledge), to holism
(rather than compartmentalization), to interpretive power (rather
than utilitarian use), to meaning as orientation (rather than
meaning as a tool, or as access to social power)—was not closer to
the traditional liberal arts or literary view of the academy than to
more contemporary standards of the academic, which, adapting
to the perceived norms and criteria of late-twentieth-century
society, have become increasingly technological. In this context,

one should not forget that traditionally the academy not only has stood for the dominant civilization and contributed to its continuity and dominance, but also has had an equally strong and equally legitimate tradition of being antagonistic to it. Its continued life may depend on its ability to preserve the tension between these irreconcilable cultural functions, in a continued search for fruitful paradox; and in our time the criticism of indigenous literatures may play a significant role in this endeavor. (It goes without saying that criticism of such writers also has more direct political functions in helping to inject knowledge of their works into the widest possible public discourse and in contributing to knowledge about them among Native groups themselves.)

At times I have believed that my own outsider status, as a European approaching Native literature in North America, constituted a decisive advantage in establishing alliances between the academy and Native cultural activities. I have had to revise that opinion, not least in the course of these interviews. In point of fact, the outside observer may be burdened in ways that are complementary to the handicaps of the inside critic. Stereotypes of otherness—be they positive (paradigm: the Noble Savage) or negative (paradigm: the Ignoble, or Beastlike, Savage)—serve as counters in games of self-affirmation, self-aggrandizement, or even self-healing played by the cultural majority, and certainly this function is more easily recognized by an outsider. Insofar as they claim to represent self-evident aspects of reality, such stereotypes assign to minorities the status of groups that may be at least semiotically, and often materially, exploited. To the critic who places him- or herself inside North American civilization, they may appear as self-evident terms of analysis. The outsider, whether she or he really comes from without or only pretends to do so in an act of heuristic self-invention, has to destroy their self-evidence and make them the objects of critical attention. We "have to" do so perhaps not so much for the sake of simple truth as for reasons of discursive sophistication and integrity. The truth of experience is very weak in combatting stereotypes, which will always reassert themselves against it. Perhaps more important, it is possible to employ a lot of truth(s) in a context that is exploitatively stereotypical: Kevin Costner's *Dances with*

Wolves has perhaps been the paramount example in the 1990s. Stereotyping in its most insidious form has less to do with truth and falsehood than with the use(s) of truth.

What outsiders may recognize more readily is the inscription of power in culture. From their critical perspective, it is either unsophisticated or dishonest not to make the power differential between a minority and the majority a theme, not only in discussions of power in society but also wherever one deals with minority cultural productions. This is the point where the deficits of the outsider position become apparent: by definition, and particularly in such moments of recognition, being an outsider implies a degree of alienation and thereby closes off access to the all-embracing "we"position that the insider will almost automatically and quite naturally adopt. In dealing with American Indian literature, insiders may be better positioned to recognize a project of Americanness shared by many (though not necessarily all) American Indians and by many other Americans as well, and shared in a manner that aspires to be egalitarian, so as to make of it a way, too, of dealing with the power problem. It seems to me that the insiders will have to mediate this sense with some recognition of historical guilt—that is, of that destructiveness of power that is more fully or exclusively acknowledged by the outsider—if they do not wish merely to continue a colonialist enterprise. But such mediation, although it may modify the sense of "we"-ness, will certainly not deny it.

Outsiders, on the other hand—and particularly Europeans—will correspondingly at least have to try to understand the existence of that shared project as a limitation to their horizon. They also need to do what some of them signally fail to do, that is, acknowledge the similarity between colonialist history in North America and colonialist history elsewhere, in which European cultures are deeply implicated. But with this qualification, which should help one to avoid self-righteousness, the European tendency, it seems to me, will always be to give precedence to the fault line, the gap of difference, within an encounter between minority and majority, which the American observer may overlook or bridge while enmeshed in the processes and contexts of acting out a sense of "we"-ness. Briefly, it seems fruitful to me for European critics, because they are by definition outsiders, to position themselves as such. This is what I have consistently done in these interviews.

The notion of power thus is pervasive at least in the background of these interviews. With all the privacy that they also have about them, the conversations constitute a type of public sphere, a Habermasian "Öffentlichkeit" that reflects on itself in an enlightened manner and that, in doing so, questions what powers are at work in it and how to theorize and regulate them and their interaction. The question belongs within a wider context: that of the mind's attempts to come to terms with and to humanize power. (Kenneth Burke's notion of a purification of conflict in and through discourse comes to mind.) The discursive shape of the interviews was determined by such an attempt just as much as is their content. This becomes particularly clear where the issue of authority—the writer's, the text's, the critic's, the audience's—arises.

Writerly authority, even as it is used for purposes of liberation, may borrow some of its means and manifestations from the majority culture against which it attempts to work, thus replicating its ways. Paradoxes like these lie behind some of the hesitations one may sense at certain points in the interviews. The peculiarly consensual effects even of the sharpest dissent, as well as the ease with which contemporary information societies coopt and commodify dissent, are by now being recognized so routinely that the very reality of the difference between consent and dissent is in danger of being lost. The interviews, to my mind, while implicitly accepting the resulting paradoxes of enmeshment and emancipation, explicitly also insist on the validity of the distinction between consent and dissent. In different but comparable ways, the authors in this context use variants of a notion of skeptical questioning: their authority in a large measure is the authority to question and criticize, where that of the dominant culture is primarily in the mode of assertion. Sociolinguists remind us that to ask questions has something to do with authority. If "the Gonja of West Africa regard questioning as a way of asserting authority over another person, so [that] it is considered inappropriate for a pupil to ask his teacher questions," as R. A. Hudson's *Sociolinguistics* tells us,[4] this is only a very strong manifestation of a general pattern. To ask questions both requires and creates a type of authority.

Such an attitude of questioning is appropriate to the era of profound change in which particularly the creators of "new" literatures find themselves. Originating in a sociocultural situation that is, in manifold ways, burdened by past and present exercises and experiences of power, the writers face unprecedented problems of legitimation. And the notion of literature itself, and of literary value, has to be negotiated anew in their works. What used to be, or appear as, a very (perhaps overly) well-defined and monolithic cultural institution has become multiple in several ways that are most apparent perhaps in an "author" like Harry Robinson. More perhaps than many others, he has made us recognize those changes in the very notion of literature that are in reality occurring all around us and that are perhaps most patent in the multiplication of audiences and modes of reception. As a traditional storyteller he had his traditional audience, whom he directly addressed; through those texts that have emerged from his interaction with ethnologist Wendy Wickwire, he indirectly addresses others that will read him. Thus Harry Robinson has at least three types of audience—in most reductively schematic terms, the community reached orally, Native audiences reached in writing, and non-Native audiences, both academic and nonacademic. All of them will read his texts differently. And so will, within the academy, readers from those various disciplines that compete for the texts as objects of study: between strictly literary readers, scholars in Native studies, and anthropologists and ethnologists, conflicts will arise over methodology and theory that are nothing but disagreements about what constitutes a proper reading of a text.

Harry Robinson may himself have separated the audiences in his own mind and practice, for example, by reserving certain kinds of material for oral presentation in Okanagan (rather than English) and within his community (rather than in exchanges with anthropologists). On the other hand, by demanding certain activities of *every* reader, his written texts also unite the various audiences into a single one. In order to make the texts comprehensible at all, one

4. R. A. Hudson, *Sociolinguistics* (Cambridge: Cambridge University Press, 1980), 101.

needs to recreate imaginatively the context of the storytelling event of which the writing is indeed, in a sense, only the trace or score. The oral event, with its specifically cultural and (above all) generally situational implications, needs to be reconstructed mentally in ways that remind one of Dennis Tedlock's ethnopoetic methodologies, though obviously such readerly praxis need not be theorized at all. It is enough that the event happens in the mind. At the same time, it cannot, by definition, happen fully again in the way it once happened; having once taken place, it is gone forever. There may be some gain to offset this loss, in that the oral event becomes the permanently available horizon of potentially innumerable acts of individualized reading.

Such changes do not constitute a disruption of history. Most obviously, they do not mean, as is sometimes still being charged, that the criticism of new literatures will have to rely on political or sociological criteria. Rather, it can—but it also will have to—develop its own properly literary criteria (which may ultimately not even be so very different from other twentieth-century criteria) out of notions of difference, interculturality, liminality, legitimation, and emancipation. One can, I believe, try to mediate these with traditional notions of literary value, even if at first sight they seemed to exist primarily in opposition to them. At the very least one will find in these interviews that the desire for change, which on the one hand leads to a shift in criteria of evaluation, is, on the other hand, based on or connected with an endorsement of the value of literature as an institution that has strong connections with the past.

Change has here been accepted as a given in yet another sense. These interviews do not privilege traditional sources. They define the primary systemic context for American Indian texts as neither monolithic nor exclusively grounded in the past, nor as in any sense essentially different or radically "other," either. I myself regard the interculturality of most contemporary minority writing as axiomatic, and the notion of the intercultural has indeed emerged from the interviews in various ways. Notions of translation, for example, recur, and so does the metaphor of the cross-blood and related notions of intercultural communication and conflict. At the same time, tradition, one has to acknowledge, does occur in contemporary indigenous texts in many different ways, some of them paradoxical. The old and the new can become one, preservation and innovation can merge in one act of expression, as they do, for example, in James Welch's acts of naming, which Robert F. Gish has characterized in the following way: "Part of Welch's technique . . . [in *Fools Crow*] is as much linguistic as it is stylistic in that he invents his own scheme of naming which, whether real or an approximation, has the intended effect of establishing an older (but for the reader newer) way of knowing."[5]

Finally, if the discussion of American Indian literature here always refers to the potential for innovation that is undoubtedly present in interculturality, it also recognizes a counter-impulse to stake claims to what is and always has been one's own. The discussion of the relation between the oral and the written, or orality and literacy, exemplifies this conflict. "Oral" has almost become a synonym for Indian (or tribal), as "written" is for white, and the dichotomy is routinely used to articulate difference. Yet the three authors and oeuvres here represented may be seen to stand (metonymically) for a pervasive and self-evident claim of Indians to make use of all the media of modern civilization; their wish to communicate that sense of difference today and all over the world subverts all simple dichotomies, and thus also this one. This may account for an ambivalence toward the opposition of oral versus written that is occasionally perceivable in the interviews, and in criticism in general. Such ambivalence may further have to do with a tendency in discussions of orality, and particularly in pleas for its renewal or revival, to replicate at least subliminally an evolutionary myth that pits original savagery against advanced civilization. Even without such Darwinist associations, the story of an evolution from orality to literacy tends to essentialize cultural difference, so that we end up having a culture (or cultures) of orality and a culture (or cultures) of literacy. This happens in positive evaluation, as in Paul Lauter's programmatic statement on "The Literatures of America," where he postulates a linear (and apparently necessary) progress from the oral to the

5. Robert F. Gish, "Word Medicine: Storytelling and Magic Realism in James Welch's *Fool's Crow*," *American Indian Quarterly* 14, no. 4 (1990): 349–54 (quotation, 351).

written.[6] It also happens where the transition from oral to written is negatively characterized in terms of total loss, as it so frequently and aggressively is in ethnopoetics.

As Carrier has pointed out in his essay on "Orientalism," though "making sense of [the] difference [between cultures] in terms of paired, dialectically generated essentializations may be understandable, or perhaps even unavoidable, . . . [i]t can lead to an exaggerated and even false sense of difference. Difference itself can become the determining, though perhaps unspoken, characteristic of alien societies."[7] If the interviews did not operate only in terms of static oppositions of the oral and the written, that was because of our pervasive attempts to avoid "dialectically generated essentializations" of the indigene and the dominant civilization. Insofar as we momentarily and (it seems to me) judiciously also made use of such oppositions, the interviews testify to the strategic usefulness of precisely such essentializations and dichotomies in communications that are unavoidably conflictual, shaped and burdened as they are by a history whose knowledge forms the horizon before which the attempt to communicate is made.

6. Paul Lauter, "The Literatures of America: A Comparative Discipline," in A. LaVonne Brown Ruoff and Jerry W. Ward, Jr., eds., *Redefining American Literary History* (New York: Modern Language Association, 1990), 9–34.

7. James G. Carrier, "Occidentalism: The World Turned Upside-Down," *American Ethnologist* 19, no. 2 (May 1992): 195–212 (quotation, 203).

The Questions

Do you find it problematic in any way that I, as a non-Indian academic, am doing these interviews?

We tend to discuss American Indian literature in terms of a group literature, or a constitutive relation between a group, "its" authors, and "its" literature. How useful do you find the notion? How much cultural "separatism" is necessary to establish a literature?

How useful do you find the notion of a world literature? How "universal" should literature be in your view?

How important to your writing is concrete factual knowledge (traditional, sociological, linguistic, etc.) about any Indian group (and/or knowledge directly derived from within that group)? How much "ethnographic" knowledge do you expect from your readership?

How much of an Indian audience do you expect for your books? Can that audience be specified?

How important to you is endorsement of your texts by an Indian audience?

What sort of reaction do you expect from non-Indian readers?

Do you specifically, in your own mind, address white readers through some of your texts? With what sort of intention?

How clear an image of your readers do you have in your mind as you write? As you (re)read your own texts? As you read other writers' texts?

What do we mean when we speak of a literature—for example, an American Indian literature—in a time when borders between cultures seem to have become permeable, and when wholes ("the canon," "society") seem to have crumbled into multiplicities?

What is the relation between specific (local, tribal) notions of Indianness and more universal notions of the indigene, or nativeness? Do you see the notion of the indigene undergoing a process of internationalization?

What, for example, do South Pacific authors mean to Indian writers, and vice versa?

If we assume that all people and groups of people have a need for stability and for change, how do (can) notions of Indianness or indigenousness accommodate this double need?

How does your writing encounter (counter? subvert?) the ethnic stereotypes that are current in the culture at large? Do you recognize differences between your writing and that of other authors in this respect?

How important is topography to your writing? How closely is it linked to notions of the land?

In reading indigenous writing, does one need to apply aesthetic values other than those one applies in reading "majority" literature? How do you react to the charge that the attempt to create or represent concrete values has in some indigenous texts produced a degree of sentimentality?

How does an Indian author deal with attacks on the authenticity of his/her "Indianness"? When and how does a writer (have to) contest other writers'/artists' conceptions of "Indianness"?

How does one react as a writer to the question of art and exploitation, and specifically to the charge that one exploits in one's writing the cultural heritage of groups within which many individuals are mentally or physically starving?

How do you react to the question of academic knowledge and exploitation, and specifically to the charge that academics exploit the cultural heritage of groups within which many individuals are mentally or physically starving?

On what does one base one's authority as an artist (and/or as an academic)?

What authority does one have?

How would you write (or tell) the (hi)story of Indian writing in North America? Where are the beginnings? What are the major phases?

How—if you accept that *House Made of Dawn* stands at the beginning of a Native American renaissance—do you account for the seminal importance of the work?

What has been the role of non-Indian critics in forming and establishing Indian writing as a viable enterprise? What (if any) influence have they had on your writing?

Do you see any consistencies, any dominant tendencies, in the representation of non-Indian people in Indian writing?

Some of my students have been worried by the representation of women (notably, but not only, white women) in Indian texts, which they have called chauvinist. Any reactions?

How important is the representation of women to the creation of a sense of difference in Indian writing?

Do you find that Indian writing is characterized by writerly mechanisms and strategies that clearly differentiate it from non-Indian writing? Are you conscious of having used such strategies yourself, or encountered them in specific other Indian authors?

A lot of indigenous writing all over the world is becoming, so to say, poly-traditional. Would you apply the term to your own writing?

Which traditions of writing do you see at work in your texts? Do you accept a label such as "realistic" or "modernist" or "postmodern" for your writing?

What mechanisms do you see at work to bring those various traditions together in single texts? What are their principles of unity?

Which so-called Western (in the sense of "majority") traditions have you specifically found useful in your writing? What would you regard as specifically Western traditions?

Which so-called indigenous traditions have you specifically found useful in your writing?

Do you find specific forms of Western writing less useful than others?

Do you find certain Western genres useless for Indian writing?

Some Indian writing seems to have avoided the straightforward use of traditional Western genres; it seems to have adapted them to its own uses, or gone towards transgressions of the conventions of such genres, or towards genre mixture. Why?

Are you interested in the (idea of) borders between different kinds of literature, such as fiction and nonfiction, fiction and poetry—either as a writerly or as a critical tool? Where do you locate the borderline between literature and other writing, or that which is "not yet literature"?

The multiplicity of frameworks of meaning alluded to in indigenous (and other contemporary) writing creates a type of "overdetermination" that makes reading difficult. What are the implications—for your own writing and for the literature in general?

Literature and criticism seem to have come much closer to one another today than in former days. What is your reaction to this development?

How do you react to the manifold ties between creative writing and the academy?

How do you react to the use of literary texts as educational tools?

Is the split between those literary texts that manage to become textbooks (on whichever level) and those that do not a decisive factor in the development of Indian literature?

How good a criterion of aesthetic value is teachability?

What other criteria would you like to see being employed in forming a canon of Indian literature—for the academy or for general reading?

How necessary in the construction of a sense of group identity is the perception or assumption or postulation of historical continuity? How much of a knowledge of "the construction of identity" can one bear in living, speaking, or acting?

How important is the recovery of lost texts?

How important is it that contemporary texts recover or reconstruct a (sense of the) past?

What in your view is the relation between a sense of the past and a sense of the future? Are they as clearly linked (mirror-fashion) as people tend to think, so that the one presupposes the other?

The theme or subject of many Indian texts lends itself to treatment in sociological, economic, or narrowly political terms, but the treatment usually does take place in broadly cultural ones. Why?

Do you accept the distinction between art and propaganda? If so, where do you locate your own texts with regard to the border line?

If we talk about the past, or history, we immediately encounter at least the possibility of radical cultural differences in perception. What, in your view, are "Indian," what are white, images of history and ways of talking about it?

How good is the publishing situation for Indian writers these days?

What is your reaction to the literacy debate?

What has happened to pan-Indianism?

What made you a writer?

How much of a sense do you have of the writer's life being different from that of "normal" people? Who are the normal people? What creates the difference?

Where do you see yourself going? Are you conscious of changes in direction in your writing? If so, what are they?

The important first phase of Indian writing appears to have taken place very much in a 1960s/early '70s way. How different is current writing from that earlier phase?

How do you address the question of violence in your works? Do your texts advocate an attitude towards it, a perspective?

Specifically, it seems to me that acts of violence are frequently represented as happening and emerging from a wider field of societal violence, in a manner that could cause the author to be charged with condoning it. How do you react to the charge? Where and how can the notion of justice be accommodated in this view? Does it not become so incredibly complex that it tends to vanish from view?

Do you see your protagonists as individuals or types? And how much sense does the distinction make to you? How important is it to you?

How do you constitute individuality in your texts?

Upon rereading your earlier works, have they changed in this or other respects (with regard to stereotyping)?

How useful do you find concepts like "the modern" or "the postmodern" to discussions of Indian writing?

When Vine Deloria, for example, advanced tribalism, or a type of Indianness, as notions of modernity, did he appropriate the notion of the modern for use by Indians? Or did he contribute to a (another) appropriation of the notion of the Indian by (non-Indian) modernist critics? Or did something more complicated—a bidirectional exchange—happen?

Similarly, what happens when Gerald Vizenor makes the trickster a postmodernist?

Indian writing addresses and constructs a sense of cultural difference, and it deals with questions of value. So does feminist writing, for example. Now it appears that Indian writing on the whole deals with the past and the present, and very rarely develops a (concrete or playful) blueprint for the future, the way quite a few feminist texts do. Why do you think this is so? Or is there a concrete utopia by an Indian author that I have missed? (The one exception that comes to mind—apart from pseudo-Indians like Lynn Andrews—is Hyemeyohsts Storm. Does his example suggest that Indian writing that does attempt to specify values (and forms of social organization that build on them) is so easily appropriated by a white audience eager for "meaning" that it only contributes to clichéd views of "the spiritual Indian"?)

How far do you think literature should develop concrete utopias? Do the notions of literature current in Indian writing exclude the genre of a utopia? If so, why?

ONE

N. Scott Momaday

Do you find it problematic in any way that I, a non-Indian academic, am doing these interviews?

No, I think it's entirely appropriate. I know of your interest in the Indian world and I think you are a good man to conduct such an interview.

Do you think you'd react differently if you had an Indian interviewer here? And in what way would you conceivably react differently?

I really don't know. I don't think I have been interviewed by many Indian people, and I think maybe there would be some common denominators if I were talking to a Kiowa, say—and many things would go without saying. There would be an understanding of a different kind, but—other than that—no, I don't think so. I don't see any big difference.

You have referred to a Kiowa, in particular, right now. Do you think you would react differently with a Kiowa, with a Navajo—because the Navajo of course are very important to you—or with a Jemez person?

I think there would be some slight difference because I would be, with a Kiowa, sharing our particular kind of experience. [I would] be comfortable with a Navajo interviewer too, or a Pueblo, I think; and maybe with Plains people in general—you know, not only Kiowa, but say, Lakota, Cheyenne—I'd be very comfortable.

I think that brings us close to the next question: We tend to discuss American Indian literature in terms of a group literature, which is a way of looking at literature in terms of a constitutive relation between it and a group. How useful do you find that notion?

[Short pause] I think you are right that we tend to think of Native American literature in that way, and obviously it is useful to think of it in that way to an extent. But I tend to see literature as literature, and I don't like to pigeonhole it, label it. I think literature is literature, and the very things which distinguish American literature, say, or French literature, or German literature, ought to be the things which distinguish Native American literature.[1]

Does that imply that to label a literature this or that is a sort of implicit instruction to the reader how to approach a particular text?

Yes, I think so. I think it's to say, "Look, we are going to deal with black literature now, so you must think of it as black literature, and you must gear your mind to accommodate the idea of a black literature." And to me that's delimiting, that's unfair.

So you would want readers to approach your texts in particular with as blank, almost, a mind as possible, as unprejudiced a mind as possible?

Right. I would like them to come to *my* writing without any preconceived notions, without any prejudices insofar as that's possible.

Which implies that all the instructions to the reader on how to read a text, are in the text itself.

Yes, you might say so.

You would then not be happy with notions of cultural separatism, of talking about a literature being constituted by a particular group voice that is radically different from another group's voice? I'm wondering also—if you look at European literature and the way European literatures developed—there was a period, for example, where German literature almost constituted itself by its being anti-French, by a spirit of separatism from the French literature of the time that was seen as much more advanced, and oppressively advanced, so that separatism there seemed to be necessary to constitute one's "own" literature.

I think there is a point to that, I think. . . . Yes, Native American literature by the same token is distinguished from other literatures, is different. It has its own experience and its own language, its own rhythms, and so I think there is a lot to be said for preserving the unique voice of Native American literature. But

---

1. *"To distinguish" is here obviously used in the sense of "to distinguish from everyday utterances" or "to make a distinguished form of communication," and it seems to me that from here onward we have to keep two sets of differences in mind: those that set the literary apart from other cultural activities and products, and ethnocultural ones, those that create borders between cultures and literatures. This interview changes its focus constantly from the one to the other—symptom of its addressing again and again, and more or less concretely, the question of universalism and relativism in literature.*

one can say that of every culture, and I don't think that one needs to approach Native American literature differently, say, than he approaches other literatures, but he must keep the distinctions in mind: all right, here is something written by a Native American— it represents a particular kind of experience, and a particular viewpoint, a particular world view, and those things it's good to keep in mind as you read.

Would you care to specify the particularities of world view etc.?

Yes.

Native Americans, I think, see the world as possessed of spirit, for one thing. They have a great respect for the earth and for the physical world.

I think that modern society in general tends to look at the earth, say, in a different way. It's not possessed of spirit, particularly; it's not vital, it's dead matter. One can exploit it without thinking much about future generations. That's one aspect. Another is, Native Americans have a very highly developed sense of language and a very rich oral tradition, and I think they tend to take language more seriously than most other people. They have a very highly developed sense of humor, which is not easily accessible to other people, but it is real and it can be used to great advantage, I think, in writing and speaking. There is a highly developed aesthetics. Indian children tend to know how to draw, and so the arts, the artistic expression of the Native American world, is very special and very highly developed. Those are some things that I think distinguish the genre, the literature itself.

Now—to get at it from the other side: how useful do you find the notion of a world literature in this context? I mean, is there such a thing, to your mind, as a world literature that is moving towards a shared aim, that is governed by shared aspirations? I guess I'm also after the question whether the term "literature" is to your mind ultimately everywhere understood in the same way. Should it be?

I don't know whether it should be or not. But I think it is becoming a kind of common, commonly understood term.

As the world grows smaller and there are more common denominators, I think people tend to think of literature in one way. We are coming closer to one understanding of literature than formerly. Now, whether that's good or not, I have my doubts—if I think not particularly of literature but simply of the fact that the world is shrinking and we find McDonalds all over the corners of the earth. To me that subtracts from the character of literature the variety which I think is important to it. If I think back to my school days and consider the Russian novel of the nineteenth century, it's a special kind of thing, it's not like any other literature. And to me that's good, that's vital. I think we are losing that with the advent of technology and—what is it called—the "information highway." The special character of various literatures is being lost.[2]

You are tackling the question in terms of historical process. I was actually, when I phrased it, wondering whether you would maybe react to it in terms of a universal instinct for the poetic, or something like that: a universal need in people everywhere to achieve a certain type of relation with reality and with language, or relation with reality through language. Are there two totally different levels to this question of universality?

There may be—you are right. I was looking at it from one point of view, and I am sure there are others that are equally valid. I do think, for example, to follow something you just suggested, that there is a kind of universal need for poetic expression, for something in literature that we have, and cannot have by other means. So there are common denominators; every culture needs the kind of expression that literature provides. It need not be the same thing from culture to culture, but certain parts of it must remain the same, as I see it.

How important do you think—and I am still basically within the context of Indian/white relations—how important is concrete factual knowledge about any Indian group to your own writing? I am talking about traditional knowledge, also sociological knowledge, linguistic knowledge, etc. How important is it to your writing, and how much knowledge of this type do you expect your readership to bring along?

2. *The question, which I phrased with the "world literature" in mind that was dear to the Enlightenment and the Romantic Age, is here being answered in terms of globalization and modernization. These are two different perspectives upon universalism, or perhaps two perspectives that make it clear that universalism can be very different things: that of the turn from the eighteenth to the nineteenth century at least intended to provide a shared basis (e.g., human rights) for the living-out of differences, whereas that of a globalized market economy can be seen as being predicated on the imposition of essential sameness.*

Well, I think it's probably the responsibility of the writer to provide what the reader needs in those terms. The more knowledge you have—for example, if I'm writing about a Kiowa protagonist—the more knowledge that the reader has of the Kiowa culture, the better off he is, but I don't think it's necessary to read beyond what I have written because I have tried to provide the necessary information.

There are other writers, and I am particularly thinking of Maori writers now, who very consciously these days are putting Maori terms, central Maori terms, into the text in Maori, and refuse to give a glossary, which they used to do in the past, and refuse to implicitly gloss these terms in the text, as if they were asking the reader to go and acquire the knowledge. They begin by first of all erecting a barrier and forcing the reader to cross that barrier under his or her own steam. How would you react to that?

I think it's rather clever. I like the idea of using a kind of special diction or information, and I am not quite sure that it needs to be understood, that one needs to track it down and find it out. I think it's nice that occasionally you come across something in writing that you don't understand, but you understand that it contributes something. Isak Dinesen said somewhere that it's not a bad thing that only half the story is understood, and I can go with that, I think. I think that's true. That's true. *Not* that I recommend confusion in literature, or chaos, but a little of it is sometimes provocative.

Is Hemingway with his iceberg theory somewhere in the same area, saying that the dignity of the story depends upon only one eighth, or whatever, being visible?

I suppose so. I suppose, yes, he's saying something in the same vein.

How much of an Indian audience do you expect for your books? And can you specify that audience?

No, I can't specify it, I don't know what it is. I have met a good number of Indian people who have read my work. I have no idea what the percentage is—more and more all the time, I think. Writing is still a relatively new enterprise for Indian people, but it's certainly growing rapidly. So I would expect that every generation more Indian people will read books by Indians. That's a good thing, it's healthy, and it's growing. Native American literature, so-called, is becoming a really integral part of American literature.

"Native American literature," so-called—are you reacting against the term "Native American," or against the labelling as such?

The labelling. I bridle a bit when I hear "Jewish literature," "black literature," "Hispanic literature," all of these in English— "Native American literature." That suggests a distinction that I think cannot be fairly made. One would be hard put, I think, to define Jewish literature in the context of American literature. It's just too much a part of the whole. You can't really cut it out and say, "This is something apart from this." It just isn't true.

Are you also saying that once you start carving all those so-called minor literatures out of American literature there is precious little left?

Precious little left. Anne Bradstreet. [Laughter]

I think you have already given the answer to the next question: How important is endorsement of your texts by an Indian audience to you? How necessary is that? Some authors tend to argue that basically they are spokespersons for their group, and that endorsement by that group is absolutely important to them. You have tended to argue, it seems to me, in terms of a more universalist view.

Yes, I think that the endorsement of Indian people to my writing is important but not appreciably more important than the endorsement of anyone else.

But I have also been extremely well received by Indian people. I think maybe if I hadn't been, I would not feel the same way.[3]

Exactly. Which has something to do, of course, among other things with the question of the importance of House Made of Dawn *in the so-called Native American renaissance. Shall we jump forward to that question? I have been fascinated how important this text is. How do you account for its importance? How do you react to its importance? How much of a burden is its importance?*

3. *A valid point, certainly: endorsement that is granted appears mostly in the shape of a "normal" author-audience relationship; it is endorsement withheld that becomes a problem, particularly where there is no institutionalized or habitualized way of asking for it, and perhaps to challenge its being withheld.*

[Laughs] I think, maybe, the answer to that is that it is simply timing, that it appeared at a time when the world was ready for it, in 1968. I think of the publication of *Bury My Heart at Wounded Knee* about the same time, and those two books contributed to some kind of important change in the publishing world, for one thing. Suddenly the publishing world found that it had an audience it was not aware of. So *House Made of Dawn* was fortunate in being very early in what has been called "the Renaissance." That meant a great deal. That meant a great deal. And moreover, you know, it was a story authentically set in an Indian community, the characters are Indian, and recognizably so. And all of that came together in a good way—so that's my answer to that.

As to how comfortable I am with the success of *House Made of Dawn*: very comfortable. It was a little hard to follow that act, you know, because here a first novel, and a first novel by an Indian, was given a major prize, and I suddenly was inundated with junk mail and invitations to speak to ladies' garden societies and colleges, and, oh yes, invitations to write—I didn't have to worry about publish-or-perish principles after that. So it was a great blessing, the acclaim, and also something of a burden, but, you know, this was something that I lived with and I think I'm past the blockage that those things can sometimes cause.

I'm pleased with it. The acclaim is very gratifying to me.

Do you specifically, in your own mind, address white readers through some of your texts? Are there certain texts or certain portions of texts that are more clearly addressed to a white readership, and if so with what sort of intention?

You know, I'm inclined to say, "Yes, certainly, I pitch part of my writing to non-Indian readers"; but I'd be hard put, I think, to make clear that distinction. I'm often asked, "For whom do you write, are you writing for an audience, or are you writing for yourself?" and I don't know. I'd like to feel that I'm writing to write. You must be familiar with. . . . William Gass was once asked that question. He said, "I don't write for myself; that would be self-serving. I don't write for a public, because that would be pandering. I write for the thing that is trying to be born." Which is probably the best answer to that question that I have heard, and I find when I sit down to write I really don't visualize a reader. It has to please *me*. So in that sense I'm writing for myself.[4]

And I'm hard to please, I think: I have to go over something until it sounds right to me, and sometimes that's a long process and a very concentrated one. It works.

Do you enjoy the process of rewriting, of revising?

Yes, I do, because I can see the difference it makes. That's always gratifying. I find it gratifying to write something down for the first time, to compose a draft, as well. I enjoy that. And then going over it, and getting something better from it—that is also gratifying.

Do you work in longhand? On a typewriter or on a computer? Do you keep previous versions?

Yes. Not all the time do I keep the drafts and the sketches.

I work very little in longhand. I always keep a pad next to the computer, so that I can jot down things from time to time, and I went through a long period when I worked with a typewriter, and I thought that I would never be able to go from the type-writer to the computer, but that has happened now, and I work at a computer.

What's interesting about the computer is, of course, the ease of revision, but also that, unless you go to particular pains, the previous versions vanish. You are always with the last version and the preceding one, the immediately preceding one.

That's right. And in a way I hate to lose the previous versions, because they represent a lot of sweat and even blood and tears, but you are right, there can be a great advantage, I think, too. With the computer the revision is so much easier and so much faster. It's a time-saving machine.

That was a loop in our talk. I'd like to go back to the question about addressing a non-Indian audience. Can I ask you about a specific scene, or actually a specific character in House Made of Dawn? *I have always*

---

4. *Was the question phrased too simply? Is there a sense in which the writer, in the act of writing, cannot but write for the sake of writing, even though outside (before, beside, beneath, after) that act other motivations may be equally strong: to improve the world, to teach, to vent one's anger, to make money, whatever? Perhaps one cannot ever get at the interaction among such motivations in a general way, but only by talking about a specific text, and reading the interaction in the traces it may have left in the text.*

wondered whether in writing about Martinez you were not particularly addressing a non-Indian audience: writing about the sheer aggressiveness of that particular character, which is of course built into white society, in a way—writing about it in a spirit of what actually constitutes virulent satire, or something like that.

I don't think of it that way—subconsciously I may have had something of that kind in mind, but, no, I think it was appropriate to take a figure of a party like Martinez, and one who is also vicious and completely prejudiced, because that has been the experience, for generations, of the Indian. Martinez—I didn't mean to single out the Hispanic character as such; it might have been, God knows, another kind of person. . . .

But one has always read him as white. . . .

Maybe. Certainly there is that: he *is* white, and Abel is a victim—but I didn't have in mind setting the Hispanic world in opposition to the Indian world, specifically.

You just used the phrase "vicious and completely prejudiced." What is the source of evil in your texts?

The source of evil? [Dramatically] "Ah, who knows where evil lurks. . . ."

Evil, I guess, in *House Made of Dawn* especially, is unknown. You know it exists in the Indian world in the form of witchcraft, and God knows it exists outside that world in various other forms, maybe innumerable other forms. I think of evil as something that is persistent in the world and unidentifiable. You can't say, "This is the definition of evil"—surely if you do that, you exclude too much. But evil *is*, evil does exist, at least in the minds of the people I write about, and in mine.

I like that phrase "vicious and completely prejudiced" because prejudice certainly exists in a social/sociological realm, whereas "vicious" can be interpreted metaphysically. So that you actually have these two sides in there.

Right.

As you reread your own texts, do you suddenly have an image of a potential reader in there, next to you?

Certainly not a clear image. I don't have the view or the vision of a particular person holding my book up and reading it. I don't bring it down to that sharp a definition. If I think of a readership it's very general. Almost, though, I don't think of the reader at all.

As you read other writers, do you feel, "Oh, they write for different readers than I do"? Has that ever occurred to you? I mean thinking, for example, of Gerald Vizenor?

I think so, yes, certainly there are some writers who are clearly in my mind writing for a readership that I am not.

Clearly, his appeal is to, as I feel, a very sophisticated reader, one who appreciates the inside jokes in Jerry's work, that particular wit that is very sharp and very distinguished, I think. His writing is very different from other writings. I think of someone like. . . .

Herman Melville, for example, in, say, *Pierre*, is writing not for an audience that I am writing for, but for some other kind of audience. There are certain writers you can pick out and say that about, but for the most part I have a hard time distinguishing.

What do we mean when we speak of a literature—for example, an American Indian literature—in a time when borders between cultures seem to have become permeable and wholes seem to have crumbled into multiplicities?

I think that's true, that barriers are breaking down, and I think that's healthy, that's good. I'm not comfortable, as I say, with isolating.

What is the relation in your mind between specific, that is, local or tribal notions of Indianness, and universal notions of the indigene or of Nativeness? An alternative way of asking that is, Do you see the notion of the indigene undergoing a process of internationalization? I'm asking that because it seems to me there are more and more international conferences—writers' conferences and other conferences—that bring together indigenous people from various parts of the world and that clearly try to define a shared project.

I feel that that's healthy in a way. I also feel that it's risky in the sense that we lose something when we dilute cultures. We lose something of the identity of a given culture, something of the specificity of being a Lakota man, for example, or a Hopi man. And the same is clearly happening within the Indian world. Tribal barriers are breaking down, and there is perhaps a growing sense of Indianness, most evident, I suppose, in the tremendous number of powwows we have now and the trading of traditions, which I think is good. Young people trade languages, and they trade songs, they trade dance steps, and so on. I find that positive, and it's also happening in music now, on an international basis.

I don't know what it all means. It's healthy to a point, and then it begins to become confused, I think, and so maybe you can carry that too far, you know.[5]

You are arguing in terms of (cultural) content. Could one also argue in terms of situation—that maybe for certain situations the notion of a shared Nativeness is more useful? I'm thinking in terms of a rough division as, for example, between the political and other situations?

I think there is great good in sharing values, traditions, whatever, among people of very different experiences. What comes to mind immediately is that we are about to mount here at the Institute of American Indian Art an exhibit of Australian aboriginal art and Native American art, and I am sure that we are going to see a lot of interesting parallels, comparisons. I think that's all to the good, to the extent that such an exhibit also makes clear the distinctions between the cultures. I think that's all to the good, too, and both things must be preserved.

It must be thought about rather carefully because one can create an imbalance and a confusion.

Do notions of colonialism, postcolonialism—conflict—enter this particular discussion at any point?

If I understand you, certainly they do. If we think about the boarding school system, for example, Native American boarding schools. Colonialism is a very destructive force in that context— Fort Marion, Carlisle, all of those places.

So that, for example, a shared attack against that particular system would be a valid sort of aim for various groups.

5. *The term "healthy" recurs. Can cultures be healthy or unhealthy? What makes for the one or the other? How does one judge? Who judges?*
What would be a better term? Would the word "appropriate" perhaps do? We are talking about a positive evaluation of the way a culture works. I want to be sure that the Gourd Dance remains a place where Kiowa culture is celebrated and you hear the language and so on. When that begins to disappear as an entity, that bothers me. It worries me a bit.

Yes. It is a common experience, within limitations. I'm sure that the Australians, that is, the Aborigines, have the same sort of colonial experience, and to compare the two may be very useful and may be very natural and logical.

What, for instance, do South Pacific authors mean to Indian writers, and vice versa? I think I should phrase that specifically. It's a question that comes out of my personal interest in South Pacific authors, in Maori and Samoan authors. Have you personally come across any of those writers, like Witi Ihimaera, Albert Wendt, Patricia Grace, Keri Hulme?

I myself haven't.

Are you aware of any status they may have among American Indian writers and American Indian audiences?

I don't recall ever having talked to an American Indian about those writers. I don't know to what extent they know them.

I find that interesting because in Canada—it may be the old Commonwealth connection—in Canada there seems to be greater awareness among Indian writers of what's going on down there.

If we assume that all people and groups of people have a need for stability and a need for change, then how can notions of Indianness accommodate that double need? It's probably a truism to say that a group can only establish a sense of its own identity if it accommodates both, notions of stability and notions of change, because if it is just stability you seek, you cut a part of yourself out of history.

I think you have to understand that stability *is* change—the only constant is change—and I think that virtually all Native Americans have a history of great change. If you think just about the Kiowas, with whom I am most familiar: from the time they came on to the plains, life was constant change for them. They had to change radically in order to become a Plains people, and then, being nomadic, they were constantly going from one landscape into another, encountering different peoples, different landscapes, different climates. Change has been their survival; their adaptability has enabled them to survive.

So when we talk about preserving a heritage or a culture, this is not exclusive of change by any means. Quite the reverse. The last thing, the most dangerous and destructive thing that the Indian can do, is to remain static, become a museum piece. So when we talk about preserving the culture we are really talking about change.

Where do certain traditions come in that people try to go back to, that they try to revive in some instances? Where do all of the traditions come in that you yourself clearly wish to preserve?

Where do they come in? What do you mean?

Are these ultimately elements of stability that sort of underpin that change that you've talked about, not in the sense of being frozen in one manifestation, but in the sense of establishing connections with the past, of preserving a sense of self-identity at the same time that you have a sense of changing identity?

That is not an easy question to answer.

I am also asking the question because I know that some authors in some areas are going to the ethnographic material because they feel there is not enough of this connection with the past.

I agree. I think we are losing our connections to the past, and *that* we must not do. And one of the ways in which we can avoid that particular danger is by preserving what we have, say, of oral tradition. The Native American oral tradition is very rich, but it is very tentative and vulnerable. Much of it has been lost, much is being lost. The good news is that we are aware, becoming more aware of how important it is and more determined to preserve it. So real attempts are being made.

I remember, as perhaps you do, that some years ago if you tried to find an anthology of Native American writings or oral tradition, you would be hard put to find two or three. Now they are all over the place, and that's good. Some of them are quite responsible, I think. So that we do have a sense of oral tradition now that we didn't have, I think, twenty-five, thirty years ago, and I can't think of a better source of cultural information than the oral tradition, the songs and stories and prayers.

You know, when I was a graduate student, I was taught that American literature was derivative of English literature and that it began in the sixteenth century or the seventeenth century in New England. And then I was asked to write a chapter for the *Columbia Literary History of the United States*—the first chapter, in fact—and I did a very brash thing: I set the origins of American literature back two thousand years. And I think that the more we learn of Native

American oral tradition and its richness, the more we have to change our idea of American literature. And that's exciting, that's revolutionary.

A lot of the oral tradition is of course preserved in writing. . . .

More and more.

What happens. . . . In thinking of the older texts, particularly of ethnographic texts, we all know what happened to the oral production, the oral performance, in its being set down in writing: how much was lost, how much was reformulated, how much was systematized.

We know?

I think we can guess that things were abbreviated.[6] For example, repetitions were taken out of the texts, and things like that, to make them appear more consistent with modern-day writings. So—how real is the preservation of the oral tradition in these written texts? Is it possible to reconstruct a real sense of the oral tradition, and what does it take to reconstruct that sense?

I think it's possible to preserve the essence of the oral tradition in writing by transcribing it. Certainly it changes, certainly something is lost. Perhaps something is gained. I don't see any good way to measure that. We don't have any way of knowing what this process really involves and what it costs.

I believe that there are very valuable and accurate transcriptions from oral tradition. Even early on—we are talking about early ethnographers—I think Washington Matthews's texts from the Navajo are quite responsible, and the Navajos that I talked to about these texts agreed. I guess to put it in a nutshell, I think there is such a thing as a *good* translation, and when you say something is inevitably lost in translation, you can't argue with that, but you can say, "Yes, but the spirit is there."

So you would not accept the argument that the only authentic production was the original oral performance, and that all processes of putting it into writing, translating it into another language, etc., etc., automatically entail a decisive loss of authenticity?

---

6. *A cautious statement, because* concretely, *of course, we usually cannot know how stories are abbreviated. But we can observe the reduction that occurs as an oral performance is* today *being set down on paper. The problem remains that we may see (or wish to see) this as a loss or as a shift, a transformation, that is, as we reflect on how the specific features of the written text may compensate for the losses.*

I think the keyword is "decisive" there. That's right, I would not. We are talking about two different things: We talk about the recitation of a prayer, say, in Navajo, by a medicine man, and it's an oral performance, necessarily. That is one thing, and it is certainly unique; it is a unique performance and cannot be duplicated. But when you talk, on the other hand, about the translation, the transcription, we've got another entity. And what I am saying is, the one can be a very good reflection on the other.

The important thing then is to accord some degree of value to alternate versions.

I think it's the only alternative. We cannot preserve the oral tradition by other means, so what we can do is be as true to it as we can and set it down in writing.

Is there a notion of survival in the background of what you are saying?

Yes, I think unless we do that, the text is lost. . . .

And all that's left is mourning, silent mourning. . . .

Yes. Yes. Right. [Brief laughter][7]

How does your writing encounter (counter? subvert?) ethnic stereotypes that are current in the culture at large? Do you recognize differences in this respect between your writing and that of other authors? What I'm after quite simply is that in the culture whose language you are using, in English, masses of ethnic and racial stereotypes have been rampant for a long time, they are written into the language. How do you deal with that fact?

By telling the truth. Someone once said of *The Way to Rainy Mountain*, "This is giving the lie to notions, stereotype notions, that are commonly held." And I think it's true that probably the best way that you can deal with those stereotypes is simply to provide the truth, and then the stereotypes fall away.

Let me ask a specific question in that context: At one point, if I remember correctly, in House Made of Dawn, *you talk about Abel standing there like a wooden Indian.[8] You remember that?*

---

7. *Are we really agreed, then, that orality, as a viable cultural way of life (or a viable road to cultural survival) is a thing of the past?*

There is a sense in which the Native American oral tradition is a thing of the past: it is less central to the survival of the culture than in the past.

8. The Way to Rainy Mountain, *chapter in the first part, "The Longhair."*

Not specifically.

That is a stereotype, of course.

Sure, yes.

You are employing the stereotype—and how can you tell the truth while employing the stereotype? This is being unfair because. . . .

No. I think it's a good question. It's called poetic license, on the one hand. And stereotypes are a part of the truth; you have to admit of their existence. And so one, I think, is free to use them to one's advantage. If you're really moving in the direction of accuracy and truth, and you can use a stereotype to speed you along, I think that's fair.

How do you use the stereotype to speed you along? What do you do to the stereotype to speed you along?

If you take that as an example, the "wooden Indian"—"Abel stood there like a wooden Indian"—there is a specific image and meaning in that. He stood there in a way that the non-Indian would expect him to stand, and they have a precedent for this stature, and it is the cigar-store Indian. So, "Why not?" I think, to my mind—and I must admit that the passage is blurred in my mind now—but if it does describe an attitude or a posture with reference to a stereotype, and it works, then that's fair game.

Actually, I think it's at a point where Angela looks at him, so that one could certainly also attribute the stereotype to her mind and to the sort of gap that exists between the two at that point. They are very much facing one another across a gap, and there is a feeling of strangeness.[9]

You know, an even better example might be Grey in *The Ancient Child* because she insists upon thinking of herself in terms of the dime novel, and she uses all of these stereotypes and clichés when describing herself, for example, as wearing tiny beaded moccasins. She thinks of her complexion as being quite wonderfully creamlike, and so on. And those stereotypes, the stereotypes of the dime novel are fascinating to me, and they work. You can talk about the character of Grey almost entirely in terms of dime

---

9. *Indeed, the passage is, "Angela thought of Abel, of the way he looked at her—like a wooden Indian—his face cold and expressionless." And then the text goes into her remembrance of the corn dance at Cochiti, which seems to her full of significance.*

novel clichés, and yet she supersedes them somehow, she comes out of that context, I think, as a real person. But it's interesting to me that she fantasizes about Billy the Kid and that she sees herself as a dime novel heroine. So I'm using stereotypes consistently there. . . .[10]

That's why I'm insisting, because I find it so fascinating that you are using stereotypes all the time, and I'm interested in what you are doing to them and what your own view is of what you're doing to them.

Well, in my view I think I'm turning the tables. I'm using the stereotypes against the perpetrators of crime as they've used them against me and have for generations succeeded. They fail to see the Indian, they see him in their own terms, and of course it's a false view. So I take the false view and throw it back.

Rather than just pretending or presuming to give the correct view?

Yes, which would be boring, I think. Which would also be a way to do it, but there is a more exciting way, and a way that is more entertaining.

Also, to my mind the problem is how, in any given language, to represent the truth without subjecting it to the danger of immediately becoming another cliché.

Always the risk, always.

In the context of this question of creating, shall we say, a more authentic image of Indianness, of the Indian, how important is topography to your writing? And how closely is the creation of topography related to notions of the land? Earlier on you used notions of the land in describing a native Indian point of view.

How do you distinguish between topography and land?

Topography to my mind would be more clearly linked to different places on the map, and to notions of journeys, distance, movement, etc. Also topography would be specific, whereas a notion of the land can be quite general, can be Mother Earth, who is basically the same everywhere. Where you've got Rainy Mountain, you've got topography.

How important is all of that?

---

10. *Would it be possible to say why it was "interesting" to you that she does so?*
Those stereotypes are a central phenomenon in American literature, and she can see herself in those terms and have fun with it.

I think in the Indian world it is extremely important. It's so basic to the world view that you have to take it into account all the time.

Particularly . . . I must go back to the example of the Kiowa migration. The topography of that journey is extremely important, and it is a part of the definition of the tribe now. I think a Kiowa in his deepest mind thinks of himself as the product of that migration, that journey, that odyssey. It would be impossible for me to think of the Kiowas without thinking of the topography and their journey. And even since they arrived in the Southern Plains, the topography of Rainy Mountain and all of those wonderful places in just that part of the world are indivisible from their experience.

In many of your works you have three main areas: the Southern Plains, Jemez, and the Navajo reservation. Would you like to talk about the way these three areas are related to one another in your works, in your life?

Yes. I could be very long-winded about that, but basically those are the three areas of my growing-up. I know those landscapes better than I know others, and so when I write, I deal with those landscapes. Sometimes I get outside them, as with Los Angeles and so on, but basically those are the three places that I know best and have chosen to write about.

The Southern Plains—I feel that I have deep roots in the Southern Plains. But I spent more time, actually, in New Mexico and Arizona. Jemez is the place where I lived during my most impressionable years, and so it is a very important place in my experience. And I got to know a lot about the place while I was there, and when I thought of writing my first novel, it seemed completely natural that I should go to that setting, which I did. The Navajo I knew as a young child, and I have wonderful memories of Cañon de Chelly and Chinle and Lukachukai, Tuba City, and Shiprock, and so I have made use of that landscape, too. I think they are all related in interesting ways: the fact that the Kiowas journeyed into Pueblo country often, and there was a real trade network; and the fact that the Navajos have a Jemez clan— they are closely related in various ways, and one of my most vivid memories of my earliest days in Jemez was the feast to which the Navajos came. There was a wonderful merger of cultures there.[11]

Can I inject a specific question here: Why does Grey have to travel from Kiowa country to Navajo country? Doesn't she recreate herself in the image of a Navajo woman? And why does Set have to have the bear experience, which I take to be a Kiowa experience, in Navajo country?

It is also a Navajo one. The bear is very important in Navajo culture.

But not the specific story of the sisters and the boy.

No, that's Kiowa. I think the quick answer to that is that Grey is preparing him, her mission is to prepare him for this encounter with the bear, and she has the advantage of not only the Kiowa lore concerning the bear, but also the Navajo lore, so she gives him the benefit of both sides of her experience and culture. So it seems appropriate that she should take him to the Navajo country, as one step in his preparation: because he is exposed there to things that he would not be exposed to if he remained in Oklahoma. So it's a process that enables Grey to work out of both of her worlds.

Why not?

I'll venture the question: Is there a sort of hierarchy in spiritual significance implied, in the sense that the Navajo world view, maybe because of its immense complexity, is the one that minds in your texts aspire to? I'm also thinking that Benally is in a way a central interpreter figure in House Made of Dawn.

I think that's a fair statement, he is.

I don't think of it in terms of a "hierarchy."

I was very much struck by the journey character of The Ancient Child. *It very much moves towards the Navajo area.*

It passes through, let's say, towards the Devil's Tower. But Grey, she is both, Navajo and Kiowa, and I wanted to realize her in both contexts, so it seemed natural to me that she would take him in the process of his apprenticeship to her people.

---

11. *So, similar patterns of linkage (here: Kiowa, Navajo, Pueblo) occur in your autobiography and in the cultural life of the groups. Isn't this a gesture you like to make, to establish parallels between the individual's and the group's life? Doesn't it also occur in* The Way to Rainy Mountain? *Does it have anything to do with your seeing yourself as a representative individual?*

I think everybody must reflect in his life the identity of the group.

Who's the protagonist, incidentally, in that book?

[Hesitation, laughter]

Is it Set or is it Grey? That's the question. I am not asking about autobiographical stories.

I think it's Set, but it's close.

A close contest?

A close contest, yes.

Have you written both of these figures as semiautobiographical ones?

I think so, simply because it's probably not possible to do otherwise. Yes, sure.

I was fascinated by the gender question because I feel that in creating Grey you must have had great fun.

It was great fun, yes. I hadn't thought about the gender aspect of it until fairly recently when I was being interviewed by someone who asked me the question, "Is Grey the female part of your own being, because there is lots of evidence to indicate that she is?" and I hadn't thought about that in those Jungian terms before, but I really suppose that she is, at least to some real extent.[12]

How does an Indian author deal with attacks on the authenticity of his or her "Indianness"? When and how does a writer have to contest other writers' or artists' conceptions of "Indianness"?

You simply write out of your experience as an Indian. If you are an Indian, then you think of yourself as an Indian and you write out of that identity. As for contesting other writers, it doesn't really come into play, I think, not at least in a conscious way. I don't ever think of myself as having to prove that I am an Indian. I think some people are in that position, and it is certainly in the field of art—painting and so on—now that there is such a controversy. But I have never had to defend my identity as an Indian and I think I have been fortunate in that to that degree. So that's not something that really shows up in my work.

12. *Quite apart from Jungian terms—is there some reflection on gender roles here, on the different ways in which males and females may traditionally have contributed to the survival of the culture, and to differences between their contributions today? Or is there quite simply a playful comment on current discussions of the gender question in academic circles and the public at large?*

I did want to pick up both concerns.

How does one determine, or who determines, who is an Indian writer?

Ultimately the writer himself, I suppose. If you are an Indian writer, if you are Jim Welch, or Leslie Silko, you write out of your experience as an Indian, and you establish your identity from the outset, and because of the peculiar relationship between the writer and the reader, the reader *believes*, takes you at your word.

So it's a question of voice, of the voice you are using.

I think so, I think that's the first thing. The second, I guess, is how convincing you are in your knowledge of the Indian world. And again, talking about the relationship between the writer and the reader, the reader goes along, that's the expectation: "Okay, if you say you are an Indian, you are an Indian, and if you tell me this in your novel I will suspend disbelief and take you at your word."

That's how it works? And what if somebody of Greek extraction, for example, writes in a very convincing manner and with a lot of knowledge?

It can be a good experience for the reader, as in the case of *Laughing Boy*.

Why not—why not a Greek writer? If he is moved to do such a thing and if he thinks he is qualified, why not try it? [Laughs]

You are being very generous.

Well, you know, I see a lot of ways to answer that question, and when I think, for example, of *Laughing Boy*, I think that's a fine Indian novel, despite the fact that it's written by a non-Indian. La Farge knew a lot about the Navajos, and he wrote a fairly good novel within that context of the Navajo world. It's convincing, it's authoritative, the voices are believable, and if someone can do that, what more can you ask of him? It's a legitimate novel, I think . . . *in Indian literature.*

And the question of exploitation doesn't enter the discussion there?

I don't think so. I don't think that La Farge was exploiting the Indian world. He was rather, to my mind, writing about something he knew well, and that's what any writer must do. He can only write out of his experience, and the valid parts of La Farge's experiences tally.

It is true, of course, that the Indian has again and again been used by the white civilization at large—whatever that may be and whoever that may be—as a sort of compensatory image or a repository of values that the white civilization has perceived itself as lacking. In this context, don't you think the question of exploitation does arise in the sense that you freeze another group in the stereotype, for example, of "the spiritual Indian," and as a writer you make your own reputation exploiting that image?

Oh, yes. I have a hard time making that case with *Laughing Boy.*

Yes.

But with other works, yes, I think so, especially where betrayal is involved.

In what sense?

That you are disclosing aspects of the Indian world that are very private and secret. Anthropologists have been doing that for generations, as you know. And that, it seems to me, is a very serious matter, and a criminal matter.

But God knows there are such works, there are things on various tribes that have been mined with bad intentions and published against the will of the Indian people. That, of course, is not to be tolerated.

Which leads us straight into the next question: How does one react as a writer to the question of voice and exploitation, how does one react specifically to the charge that one exploits in one's writing the cultural heritage of groups that are in many instances made up basically of disadvantaged people?

I think maybe it comes down to definition, it comes down to a kind of semantics. Exploitation—what is the difference between "exploitation" and "celebration"?

I think when I write about the Kiowa world, as in *The Way to Rainy Mountain,* that I am engaged in an act of celebration, I'm celebrating that experience. One could argue that I'm exploiting the experience, that I'm taking something from my own heritage and turning it to my advantage—exploitation in that sense. I don't see it that way, and I think that questions of that kind—the difference between exploitation and celebration—arise constantly not only in literature but in the visual arts and even in ceremonial arts, dance and performing arts. I think where exploitation really—in the commonly accepted definition of that word—exists it's fairly easily recognized, or recognizable. When someone, for example—a non-Indian—obviously paints in an Indian style and represents himself as an Indian artist, that's exploitation of that kind.

But the difference between that and, say, Leslie Silko writing *Ceremony*, which is I think a celebration, *that* distinction is fairly easy to see even if it isn't easy to explain.

Good question, though—lots of food for thought in that question.

How do you react to the related question of academic knowledge and exploitation? How do you react specifically to the charge that academics like myself exploit the cultural heritage of groups within which many individuals are mentally or physically starving?

I think that one has to distinguish between academic work and other kinds of work. There is a difference between, say, a novelist who is telling a story and an academic who is writing a treatise or really contributing, as they say, to the world of knowledge. The two processes are similar, but they are not quite the same thing. I believe that the academic, the anthropologist, say, who goes onto the reservation, is entitled to do the kind of work that he is trained to do. Frequently he abuses his privilege—we have seen this, and again I get back to the idea of betrayal—but basically you know there is room for the anthropologist in the Indian world as there is for the novelist and the poet.[13]

People have, of course, also used notions of service in this context in the sense that the knowledge that's being collected will immediately and first of all be placed at the disposal of the particular group under consideration, for example, in land claims and things like that. But I think it's more difficult to make that sort of argument for somebody who works in literature.

Yes, that's right. That's another academic aspect, that's true.

All this has something to do, of course, with questions of authority, of the authority of one's own work, the authorization, the legitimation of one's own work. My next two questions are: On what does one base one's authority as an artist? (and/or as an academic? And of course, you are

13. *Here, I think we move from a distinction between creative and critical work to a recognition of their similarity, in which they appear as two different, but equal forms of knowledge. Can one put your views on the relation between the two forms of knowledge in a nutshell?*

These are legitimate and separate forms of knowledge. My investment is in the poet's.

both.) And what authority does one have? I have phrased that very generally, in a way, but I'm very much also thinking of you, because I have always felt that you come across as somebody who knows that he has (and who wants to have) a degree of authority.

Many things come to mind when I think of answering that question. I believe that I do have a certain authority to write about the Indian world, and it is based upon experience. I have lived a large part of my life in the Indian world, on reservations and in my own family and household, so my experience gives me a kind of authority, provides me with a subject, and it seems perfectly natural that I write out of that experience with that authority. There are so many different cases, you know: what about this guy, over here, who's writing about Zuni, and who grew up in the Bronx? Where does his authority come from? I don't know about that. He may have it, but I wouldn't know, without recourse to very special information, how he came to get it. So I can only speak for myself, and I guess that answers the question as far as I am concerned.

You would basically argue in terms of experience, rather than in terms of language and your own skill in using it? I'm asking because I have always also found that, when you are addressing an audience, you very much seem to put yourself into a position or posture of authority that has a lot to do with the way in which you are handling language.

Well, I would have a hard time differentiating language and skill from experience; they seem to me to go under that rubric all right.

I don't have a deep knowledge of any Indian language, including Kiowa. I have smatterings, you know. When I was in Jemez as a boy, I learnt to speak rudimentary Jemez that enabled me to converse with the old men in the village. I studied Navajo intensively one summer, and I heard it through some of the years in my very young boyhood. I heard Kiowa—my father was fluent in Kiowa. I hear Kiowa now when I go to the Gourd Dance, but I don't have possession of any of those languages. And yet I think I have what may be important: a sense of the way in which the oral tradition of the Kiowa, for example, emanates from the Kiowa language, or vice versa. There is something in the rhythms of the language, and that fascinates me. I've seen examples of that, people responding to the Yeibichei, the chants which are unintelligible to us mortals and yet you have to react to it because it is so intrinsically moving.

I once—this is an aside, but it's interesting to me—once travelling through central Asia, I was lecturing as I went eastward towards the Chinese border, and the farther I got the fewer people I encountered who could understand English, and finally, at the University of Dyushambe I had to have a native speaker, a Tadzhik speaker, next to me who was translating: as I read in English she would then repeat in Tadzhik. And I read a poem called "Remember My Horse," which is very rhythmical and full of repetitions; the sound of it is something in itself.[14] I read it, and before she

---

PLAINVIEW: 2

I saw an old Indian
At Saddle Mountain
He drank and dreamed of drinking
And a blue-black horse

Remember my horse running
  Remember my horse
Remember my horse running
  Remember my horse

Remember my horse wheeling
  Remember my horse
Remember my horse wheeling
  Remember my horse

Remember my horse blowing
  Remember my horse
Remember my horse blowing
  Remember my horse

Remember my horse standing
  Remember my horse
Remember my horse standing
  Remember my horse

Remember my horse hurting
  Remember my horse
Remember my horse hurting
  Remember my horse

Remember my horse falling
  Remember my horse
Remember my horse falling
  Remember my horse

Remember my horse dying
  Remember my horse
Remember my horse dying
  Remember my horse

A horse is one thing
An Indian another
An old horse is old
An old Indian is sad

I saw an old Indian
At Saddle Mountain
He drank and dreamed of drinking
And a blue-black horse

Remember my horse running
  Remember my horse
Remember my horse wheeling
  Remember my horse
Remember my horse blowing
  Remember my horse
Remember my horse standing
  Remember my horse
Remember my horse hurting
  Remember my horse
Remember my horse falling
  Remember my horse
Remember my horse dying
  Remember my horse
Remember my blue-black horse
Remember my blue-black horse
  Remember my horse
  Remember my horse
Remember
Remember

---

14. *The poem is now called "Plainview: 2." It is here reprinted with the author's kind permission from* In the Presence of the Sun *(1992).*

could begin her translation, the audience applauded, and I knew that they didn't understand what I had said, but they were responding to the rhythms of the poem. I think that's a terribly important thing in oral tradition. If a Kiowa, an elder—or a Navajo were to come and tell us a story in Navajo, we wouldn't understand it, but we might react to it, we might well react to it, respond to it, in a very favorable way.

In a way you are not talking of grounding one's authority in any of the specific languages, but in Language with a capital L. . . .

In a way, you are right. . . .

And in a certain way of using it.

I have to, you see. Because I don't understand Lakota, say, I can't talk about the importance of the language in that sense, in its meaning, its basic intelligibility; but I can talk about it in terms of its effect upon my ear, the sound of it, the rhythms, the repetitions, the nuances of inflection, and so on. And that, it seems to me, is almost a language in itself, you know, just the sound.

Which probably has a lot to do also with performance. It is not only sound, it is also the physical presence of the speaker. . . .

Yes, you are right.

And vibrations of a different sort, probably.

Yes. You have been, I'm sure, to Yeibichei dances and so on.

[Silent "No"]

You haven't?

These are Winter Dances, and the Yeis are the mountain gods, and they speak a language that mortals do not understand. And very late at night they come out of the hogan—they are masked figures—and they dance in single file and chant, and it's an otherworldly experience, the sound of the chants.

We (my wife and I) have never had this sort of connection with any Navajos that we have had with Hopis—it's very curious.

Yes. You are right in the middle of the Navajo Reservation.

If we turn to literary history, how would you write or tell the story of Indian writing in North America? Where are the beginnings? What are the major phases?

I'm not a student of Native American literature in a historic way, so there were things happening around the turn of this century that I'm not up on. If you talk about the origins I would go back to the rock paintings and say that this is an emergence of literature, that what we have here is involved in story. We don't know what the story is, but we know that it is a story, that it has meaning, and that the people who placed these images on the rock were dealing in language. They were telling stories and they were illustrating them. And so you know it's fair, I think, to talk about origins of literature in that way.

The process of evolution. . . . The oral tradition of course is the single thread that really holds it all together. From the time that the Paleo-Indians first set foot upon the continent, they were telling stories, and every generation since has had a tradition of storytelling. In our time the oral tradition has begun to enter into the written tradition, and as I say, those people who were writing in the early twentieth century took up the thread, and their voices, I think, were very weak. They are ironically becoming stronger now, because we have had a more visible written literature from about 1950.

Do you think that in the current general literary scene there are better tools available to the writer to represent the experiences that need to be represented in American Indian writing than there were maybe around the turn of the century? I'm asking because those turn-of-the century texts are, some of them, very difficult to read these days: they appear terribly sentimental, terribly false. It is as if the proper language wasn't yet available.

And I think that's true. I think that's true.

Those early Indian writers had very poor models upon which to base their work, poor in the sense that they had access more immediately to sentimental accounts. It's like poetry in the nineteenth century in America: much of it is nature poetry in the worst sense. But as time passed and as the Indian became more literate and more exposed to other kinds of writing, and better kinds of writing, he has gained a lot in the process. An Indian writer of the 1990s can be counted on to have a wider experience of literature than the Indian writer of the 1920s.

So you would argue it's rather more a question of—let's say, to put it very crudely—the education of the writer than a question of the development of literary patterns, genres, discourses, etc., through time?

I think it's both.

I think that the language barrier, if we can use that term, was a much greater impediment twenty years ago, fifty years ago, than it is now. That barrier is breaking down. More and more Indians can read and write. And that accounts for a great difference in the quality of literature.[15]

That also accounts for your belief in the possibility of good translations that we talked about earlier?

Yes.

What has been the role of non-Indian critics in this process of forming and establishing Indian writing as a viable enterprise? What (if any) influence have they had on your own writing? In your particular case I was thinking of Yvor Winters, for example.

When you asked the first part of the question I immediately thought "too much of an influence"; the critics have defined Indian literature, and I think that they in many cases have not understood what it is, and so they have created false impressions of it and they have set down arbitrary rules for defining it.

In my case the critics have been good to me by and large, but I take the criticism of my work with a grain of salt. I don't believe the favorable critics any more than I believe the unfavorable critics. They don't play much of a role in my work, I think.

Now what about Yvor Winters?

I was not thinking of him as a critic of your work, obviously, but as one of the major critics of modernist poetry who was also interested in Native American literature. What, if any, influence, do you think, did he have on the development of your writing?

Of my writing? A great deal, I think. He was a very important man in my career as a writer.

We were very close friends, for one thing; we developed a very deep friendship over the years in which we knew each other. I came to respect his literary intelligence and above all his integrity. I was talking to someone earlier today in fact about him and was commenting that he was, more than any other man that I have ever known, true to his convictions. I have never known anyone

15. *In English only, or also in Native languages?*
The visual text can indicate dimensions of the oral tradition that are not recognizable in other ways.

with as much integrity as he had. And so I admired him a great deal, and I think I learnt a great deal about poetry studying with him. When I went to Stanford I thought of myself as a poet, but as a matter of fact I knew very little about traditional forms in poetry, and so in the four years that I was there, working closely with him from the beginning, I learnt a great deal.

What did you mean by "traditional forms" just now?

Prosody. I didn't know an iamb from a dactyl, and that's the sort of thing I learnt: I learnt about iambic pentameter and the heroic couplet, the sonnet and the villanelle—all of that formal stuff which, trite as it sometimes sounds, is indispensable to a writing of poetry. You have to understand—if you write poetry in English, you have to understand something about the formation of English poetry through the centuries. And that's what I was lacking, and that's what he could give me along with other things, and so that was a very important education for me as a writer.

Did he in any way also influence your view of the connection between this English repertoire and Native traditions?

Yes, to some extent. He had experimented in his earlier career with Native American formulae, if I can use the word—expression. He had seen the translations of Washington Matthews and other people, and he wrote a series of very short, two-line (most often) pieces which reflect the rhythms of the Native American song. So he was keenly interested in that, and through the years at Stanford he had worked with students who were also interested in that and they had exchanged ideas and so on, as he and I did.

So, yes, I think he was able to point to certain parallels or certain comparisons, contrasts perhaps, between Native American expression and English poetry.

If one had to give a literary-historical label to Winters, I would probably call him a modernist critic. Are you happy with those labels? Would you on the basis of your view of poetry, language, etc., define yourself as a modernist writer?

I don't know. I don't object to that label, but I don't myself *have* a label for my work.

I don't know what those terms finally mean, you know, "post-modernist," "modern"—"deconstruction." [Laughs] I don't spend a lot of time thinking about those things or wondering where I am in the complexity of them.

Does that also have something to do with a certain tendency on your part to keep criticism and creative writing apart, assigning to yourself basically the task of the writer?

Yes, I keep those things clearly apart, and I don't think of myself as a critic at all. I'm a writer and. . . .

You are also an academic teacher. . . .

Only in a sense am I an academic. I am in that world and I have been for a long time, but I don't think of myself as being a professional teacher. I do it because it enables me to write, so the two things go together for me very well. But as for thinking of myself as one or the other—it's clearly the writer, not the professor.

What is the function of the critic? Earlier on there were those critical undertones in what you were saying about what critics have done to and with American Native literature.

I think that clearly the function of the critic is to enable us better to understand literature. A good critic, I think, will show us things in literature that we might not see for ourselves. So that's a very important function, and goodness knows we must rely upon that kind of aid in our experience with literature. But I'm not concerned really to interpret literature in that way. I write myself and I leave it to others to interpret it if they can and will.

Will you read the interpretations of critics with interest or with detachment?

Both. Sometimes I find a critic who is saying something that interests me and who is saying it in a way that enables me to think more clearly about it. I don't spend a lot of time reading criticism. It's a relatively rare experience for me and sometimes it's very profitable, and sometimes not.

In a conflict of opinions over certain texts, who has the final say what the text means, the author or the critic? The critic, I mean, standing in a way for the audience.

I suppose it can differ from situation to situation. I would say, the quick and simple answer to that is, the author. No one knows presumably quite as well as he what he is up to. That's not always true, I'm ready to admit that. Sometimes the least reliable witness to a work of art is the creator himself; but it's his intention that matters above all, what he sets out to do, that is the real test. Whether he does it or not, that is maybe up to the critic to say at last. But the critic, I think, cannot take over the authority of the author, that is sacred.[16]

A nice final word, but I may not accept it as such. . . .

[Laughs]

The next block of questions that I have is on the creation of character: Do you see any consistencies, any dominant tendencies in the representation of non-Indian people in Indian writing?

Yes, if we're talking about "modern," if we talk about writing, yes, I think that the non-Indian has been consistently a foil in Indian writings. The tables are turned in a way and the white man has become in some sense the intruder. I suppose that there has been a backlash to the creation of stereotypes on the part of the whites, and then on the part of the Indians, so you do get villains in Native American literature who are predictably white.

In this context, and in leafing through In the Presence of the Sun *this morning, I was struck by some of your very short epigrams which are quite satirical in some instances. I was wondering, would you regard it as a fair statement if one said that in part you are a satirist?*

Well, in those instances I think so, that's a fair statement.

But it's not generalizable? I was suddenly tempted by the idea of generalizing it, of reading, for example, the portrait of Angela in part as a satirical one, which would be an interesting perspective to me because you have always been read and also talked about in terms of an "image maker," which is basically a sort of affirmative function, whereas the satirist's function is always first of all a subversive, negative one.

Yes, and if you set up those categories, I see myself 90 percent in the one and 10 percent in the other. I like writing satirical things, I like parody. Those two-liners are like eating peanuts: you start doing them and you can't stop. And I like to tell the story, when I'm reading them aloud, that I began writing them in the swimming pool as I would do laps for exercise, and there is nothing more boring, so in order to combat this deadly boredom, I began

---

16. *Does the choice of language here ("sacred") indicate a feeling that this sort of writerly authority is under attack in the current climate?*

Oh, yes.

to compose epigrams as I swam, and I would come up with these two-lappers and four-lappers. And they were fun to do, and I started just writing those things as an exercise, really, to keep a form clearly in view, and they are addictive and they can be like eating peanuts.[17]

So I have a few of those in the new section.

Then the general idea of Scott Momaday as a satirist does not appeal to you?

I'd rather be thought of as something else, you know; but certainly that's a part of it. If you want to say, "Scott Momaday is a satirist," that's fine with me. I say, "Ah, but only in part, and probably a minor part."

It would raise the fascinating question precisely of the interrelation between the parts. Also, earlier on we talked about Grey. And clearly in the way in which her mind is made to use the clichés of the dime novel, there is a satirical answer.

That's right. I was about to say the same thing, but you mentioned Angela. Certainly in other of my writings there are satirical elements. Tosamah—my goodness, yes, a lot of satire.

In that context, Tosamah raises the same question in my mind that Grey raises: What's the function of satire there in a figure that at the same time has all those autobiographical aspects and that in the text also has a tremendously affirmative function? Tosamah is not just a satirized figure; he is also somebody who retells some of the central texts in your oeuvre, and he is also the one who handles language best.[18]

That's right—in the entire book. That's right.

The question is, what's the relation then between the subversive aspect of satire and those affirmative aspects that are also linked to the figure?

I suppose that the function is to create a kind of tension. Satire has a purpose, satire exists not for its own sake, perhaps, but it

---

17. *And why are they addictive? What sort of craving do they satisfy? What is it that makes for their attractiveness? Is it only the attraction of form, or also that of invective, of aggression?*

No.

18. *Tosamah's character forces one to distinguish between satire and parody in Momaday. If, indeed, Angela is a satirical figure, she satirizes an attitude that is ultimately, in the context of the novel, attacked as being destructive. Grey's parodic play with clichés is largely celebratory. In Tosamah, we may have an interesting degree of indeterminacy precisely with regard to the question, Satire or parody?*

does further other movements in a given work of literature, and as I think of Tosamah and Grey, or Angela, the satirical elements that inform them are positive in the sense that they move the action along. They contribute something to the motion and shape of the work as a whole, something indispensable. Satire functions in that way. If you talk just about the epigrams, they do in my mind seem to exist for their own sake, but as for the characters in novels, that's another kind of satire.

So that the ultimate interest then would be the movement of the work as a whole, not the creation of these particular characters as entities in themselves that sort of step out of the work.

No, I think that they must contribute to the context in various ways.

And ultimately the final category is story, not character?

Exactly.

And as I have said in several places, and clearly in *The Ancient Child*, there is *one story*, and all stories are within the one, and we are all characters in the one story, and we must be true to our parts.

Some of my students in a seminar I have just taught at Berne were worried by the representation of women (notably, but not only, white women) in Indian texts, which they have called chauvinist. Any reactions?

I don't see it.

Poor Angela?

Angela is a sick person. There are such people in the world. She moved the book along in a positive way, I think. Her attitudes towards Abel represented a reality that is important in the novel. I think of her as being an interesting, freakish sort of character, not a major character in any sense, but nonetheless an indispensable one.

I don't know otherwise how to answer that question. I think of Grey as being not only a sympathetic character but a major one, so it seems to me that the charge of chauvinism would be hard to defend in her case. Angela is something else though.

I forget the name of the other woman in House Made of Dawn.

Milly.

She's a broken figure as well, isn't she?

Yes.

The question would perhaps return then: Is it impossible in that sort of text to have a positive female character?

In that text Fat Josie is a positive figure.

We've been talking about differences between Indian writing and other kinds of writing again and again, and then we've been talking about writing with a capital W. I'd like to return to the first question: Do you find that Indian writing is characterized by writerly strategies that clearly differentiate it from non-Indian writing?

Would you recognize an Indian text "discursively," by the voice it's using, in a blindfold test?

Some of the time. It depends upon the writer. I would think that you could look at my writing without knowing it was mine and understand that it was an Indian point of view and perhaps an Indian style of expression. I think you could do that with Jim Welch. There are any number of poets you could look at and recognize their work as Indian. What distinguishes Indian writing I think is its relationship to the oral tradition, and this is true especially in poetry. Simon Ortiz, Luci Tapahonso, Ray Young Bear are all writing out of an oral tradition, it seems to me, and that is recognizable, and that is an important point of distinction. So, yes, I think ideally you could recognize an Indian text without knowing who wrote it.

Which brings me to my next question: A lot of indigenous writing all over the world is being characterized as, and may indeed be becoming, "poly-traditional," drawing on many different traditions, all of them in a sense indigenous to the particular place. In a way we talked about it in the context of your knowledge of and your immersion in the traditions of English poetry. And when you talked about the two-liners, you could conceivably also have alluded to Japanese traditions.

Yes, something like that. True.

Is "poly-traditional" a good term then?

It is a good term, I think, and as we go along, I think of the process in which the Native American writer has become a literary man. He has an investment in his own oral tradition. We hope that as a writer he is deeply immersed in that tradition, and then he discovers the written tradition, he becomes literate and he writes in English. But there is a thread, a strong thread between what he is writing and what that tradition he is grounded in represents, and that's the important thing. When I say you can recognize in Simon Ortiz, for example, an Indian quality of expression—easily—that's the relationship that I am talking about. And this shows up more obviously in poetry than it does in prose fiction. But there you can see it, too, in, I think, my work and, as I say, Jim's and other people's writing.

Would you say that one could classify American Indian prose according to its closeness to this tradition and the degree to which it moves away from it? Since you mentioned Simon Ortiz, it seems to me that in his poetry he is very close to that tradition, in his short stories he doesn't seem to be. At least quite a few of them seem to me to be firmly embedded in the western tradition of local-color writing with its socio-logical interest.

I think you are right, and this is to say what I was saying a moment ago about the difference between poetry and prose. Poetry, obviously, is much closer to the oral tradition in and of its nature.

What I'm also trying to ask is whether you'd agree that some prose texts are closer to the poetic principle and try to stick closer to the poetic process than others. Your prose, for example, much more so than other people's.

Yes. And I account for that in that way. I think that the lyrical quality in my writing is something that can be attributed to my interest in oral tradition and to the poetic principle, as you say, in that tradition.

It has always struck me, too, that a lot of your writing is not easily classified by genre. I was thinking of texts like The Way to Rainy Mountain *and* The Names. *What is the significance, what is the use of traditional genres in your own work and in Indian writing?*

I don't think that it's a matter of great importance to specify classifications, genres, and so on, in my work, and this may well be true of other Native Americans who write.

It rather pleases me, I must say, that *The Way to Rainy Mountain* has been hard to classify, and you find it on various shelves in the library, under various rubrics. I think that's in a way as it should be, because Native American writers are working out of a particular experience and it is good that they are able, I think, to write things that are not easily classified in traditional ways.

House Made of Dawn is a novel, I suppose, but it's an unconventional one, so is *The Ancient Child*. I think *Winter in the Blood* is an unconventional novel. Louise Erdrich's works are not conventional novels, I think, and that's to their credit. They exist in an area which has yet to be clearly defined; it's a departure, as it were, from traditional literary forms.

You said just now it pleased you that, for example, The Way to Rainy Mountain *has been difficult to classify. Was there also any intention to go beyond genre boundaries in writing the work? Was there any conscious attempt to not adhere to genre traditions in writing* The Names, *for example?*

It wasn't a major consideration, but it certainly was a consideration. I wanted to do something that had not been done before. I wanted to strike new ground. I wanted in the first place, and this goes back all the way to *House Made of Dawn*, to establish a kind of Indian voice, one that you don't find often, but there was the opportunity, and there was the point of view, and there was the authority, and so that's what I was trying for. That certainly was a consideration.

One could argue, of course, that House Made of Dawn *is within the tradition of unconventionality. . . .*

[Laughter]

The tradition of Joyce, Woolf, Faulkner, and all those modernists. But it seems to me that The Names *or* The Way to Rainy Mountain *cannot even be put into that sort of genealogy.*

You may be right.

Which is not to say that these are necessarily better or greater works than House Made of Dawn, *but there seems to be a firmer intention not to be classifiable.*

I don't know what the strength of that intention was when I was writing these things,[19] but I was not concerned, I can say, to follow formulaic writings in American literature, say. I was speaking out of my own voice and it was a good voice, an authentic voice. I loved to experiment more than do things that people do ordinarily do, and so I came up with unconventional

19. *Perhaps it makes more sense to say that there appears to be a stronger tendency to avoid classifiability—and this would raise the question whether there was anything in the literary-historical situation to foster such tendencies.*

aspects, have consistently—in my fiction, particularly, I think. Why not?

Is there behind your writing a very clear urge not to repeat yourself? Is it almost a vital necessity to move on to something new whenever you have written something. And if so, why?

I don't know the answer to that. I think I don't want to repeat myself in a negative sense, that is, to say the same thing again, but I have no hesitation in taking something that I have written before and building upon it in another work.

Yes.

I'm also asking the question because, before you came in, I also read the last poem in In the Presence of the Sun, *and that seemed to me to be very much a poem about the exhaustion of one thing and the need to move on to something new, again and again, as if this was one of your basic experiences: that things, phases of life, maybe people, and the personality you are at any given time, very easily exhausted themselves, so that you've got to go through a metamorphosis.*

Yes, I think that's a fair statement. That does happen and has happened to me. I do feel the need to move on from one thing to another. Sometimes it's a very needful kind of thing, crucial in a way.

Does language easily exhaust itself for you?

I find it inexhaustible.

Does any given way of speaking easily exhaust itself?

Well, I would have to think about that, but my immediate response is, yes, there are styles, there are modes of expression that become exhausted, and there is a strong feeling that I've got to move on to something else because this air is becoming very stale.

Is that one motivation for making Grey, for example, talk through the dime novel, think through the dime novel, think through cliché?

I think so. I think probably that's one way to account for her very particular commitment to that kind of expression. It's fresh. It's fresh for her, and it's fresh for me, to deal with that antiquated kind of expression. It is very much an entertainment to me as a writer. It's fun to go back to Deadwood Dick and so on—*The Authentic Life of Billy, the Kid.* Wonderful stuff.

So that parody is one way of rejuvenating oneself?

That's certainly one of its functions, yes.

I think in a way we have talked about the question of borders between different kinds of literature—how useful are they? Basically you would probably not be interested very much in genre notions, notions of this type of literature versus that type of literature. It's all "right." Is that true?

I suppose that it's basically true. I'm not concerned to categorize these things, to give them labels. They are all the expressions of the writer's spirit, and I think that expression can be made validly in any number of ways, in any number of categories, and it's more or less arbitrary to give them labels.

Anyway, I think there are uses for these things—I myself am not so much concerned with them as a writer.

Are these critical uses rather than creative uses, then?

Is it that such notions might be useful in classifying literature from the point of view of reception, but they are not generative principles so much? Which is, of course, a way in which notions of genre etc. were indeed used in the past. You sat down to write a novel, and you knew exactly what you had to do in order to produce that, and what your aspirations were.

What I'm saying is that I can understand that it's useful in certain areas to specify that *The Names* is autobiography, *House Made of Dawn* is fiction, *The Way to Rainy Mountain* is folk material of some kind, but to the writer these distinctions are not very important. If I'm writing a passage in *The Names*, I write it with the same degree of attention and concentration that I write a passage in a novel or a stanza in a poem. The distinctions to me are not so important in the act of writing. To the critic I suppose they are more important. "Let's talk about *this* corner of Momaday's activity, the autobiographical narrative; we can take this and we can distinguish it from all other things."

But I doubt that you can. If you look at The Way to Rainy Mountain, *where you've got that third item on every double page, it's only there that you've got autobiography. The text as a whole is mixed.*

That's my point: as a writer, that's fine. The distinctions are not important. It may be bothersome to the critic that he can't make these distinctions. That may be a worry, but not to me.

I don't think it has to be a worry to the critic because the distinctions still enable him or her to make statements about the text—that it transgresses the borders—and these are interesting statements. If you say that Momaday refuses to isolate the genre of autobiography from other kinds of discourses, but that autobiography does enter The Way to Rainy Mountain, *then you can make all kinds of statements that are based on that information.*

I see that and agree with it. To the librarian who is trying to find where to place *The Way to Rainy Mountain*, that's another problem.

Oh, sure.

I'd like to get into that question of literature and politics. The themes of many Indian texts would lend themselves to treatment in sociological terms, economic terms, political terms, or psychological terms: alienation *and things like that. You get all those broken characters we had earlier. Usually the treatment takes place in broadly cultural terms, terms of cultural identity, not so much in terms of the sociological.*

Why is that so? Is that a good thing? Is that potentially dangerous? Could one talk about "the culturalization of social conflict"?

One could.

I guess maybe what my response to that would be is that I, out of my personality, out of my temperament, am more interested in culture than in those aspects such as sociology and economy and so on. And so I write out of a more broadly cultural view than perhaps other writers. I don't know. I am not particularly interested in politics, or to put it another way, I approach politics very obliquely; it's not the center of my writing.

One, I suppose, cannot write without writing politically, but it's not something that I set out to do.

I think that there is a broader framework to this question that I have only just become conscious of, a framework within the terms of my own thinking, which is that it seems to me that there has been, at least for the last twenty years or so, a tendency in American literary thought in general, which includes the academy and the activity of literature, to culturalize social conflict, to talk about social conflict in terms of cultural conflict. It probably goes together with the fact that class is not a central category in contemporary literary thought and theory in the United States, but ethnicity is. Is there a tendency—this is sheer speculation, and I'm inviting you to speculate—is there a tendency in the current scene to avoid the concretely political and to displace it into the area of culture?

I really don't know. My sense is that probably, yes, there is a tendency in that direction. I don't know how well defined it is, and it's not something that I have thought about in any depth at all.

If that was the case I would wonder whether in the long run maybe young college-educated Indians, for example, may not look for other, more political means. It's also a question about the status of literature in defining the group, the group's sense of identity, and the group's sense of shared purpose.

I don't know. I think what comes to my mind is that probably the breakdown within the Indian community is about what it is elsewhere. That is to say, there is probably a growing interest in the political potential of the Indian community as much as there is in the awareness of a literary potential in the community. I don't know how you would measure those things at the moment. I know that a good many young Indian people are going into law and medicine and politics, a good many are becoming poets and novelists, and whether you can say that one field is more active than another at this point I don't know.

In this context it has seemed to me that literature has been tremendously important in undergraduate teaching in Indian colleges, in creating a sense of shared purpose, for example—and that was a context of this speculation really.

I think it's true that the Indian has a greater investment perhaps than other peoples in general in language. It has been extremely important in his history and prehistory. The oral tradition is something that has developed over untold generations, and it has been one of the principal resources of the Indian, not only throughout the great tenure of his existence on this continent but in modern times as well. It may be even more important in some ways than it was—I don't know—that's really speculation—but it certainly has new uses, it can be directed in ways it was never directed before.

It has become formalized teaching.

Yes, certainly that. It has become a kind of newly defined thing in education.

How happy are *you about the use of literature in this sort of educational enterprise?*

Oh, I'm always delighted when we can find a good use for literature. I feel very good about it, very positive. I think one of the great contributions the Indian has to make is the sharing of his understanding of language, the importance of language, his recognition of the power and beauty of language. That's something that is very important—has been, for a very long time—and in our time we suffer from what someone has called "word inflation," and we have lost a great deal of respect for language, we tend to use it carelessly. In the oral tradition one cannot, one dare not use language carelessly, and there remains, I think, in the Indian world that sense of responsibility and that respect for language, so that it's a good thing that it is carried on in the schools.

Will the schools be able to carry that on? Will the schools even be able to instill a real sense of the value of language in people who are at the same time exposed to TV?

That is a good question, and who knows? I've seen some of the results of television in my time; I was alive when it came to be, and I've seen what happens. It represents a risk, and who knows what effect it will finally have on literature, upon the understanding of language? Certainly it will have some bearing. What it will mean we have yet to find out.

I have been appalled by the decline in quality of American TV during the last five years or so. . . .

Yes, it's deplorable.

Back to literary history: The important first phase of Indian writing appears to have taken place very much in the '60s and early '70s. How different is current writing from that earlier period? Do you sense that we are in a second major phase? Are we still within the same phase as in the '60s/early '70s?

I think we have made some progress. I think Indian literature is larger and better across the board than it was in the '60s. It's very early to say what the differences are, but I'm confident that, yes, as time goes on the quality of writing becomes better, Indian people are becoming more familiar with the English language and what they can do within it. They have the benefit of what has gone before, so they have something upon which to build. So it's becoming better, I think, stronger.

What would be the relation between literatures in the indigenous languages and anglophone Indian literature, in your mind?

I think it's basically the same thing as trading songs, as happens among young people at powwows these days. There is room in all of these tribal dimensions for new blood, so to speak, and why not in the realm of literature as well? Certainly, I think that as the world becomes smaller, and as there is more contact between and among Indian communities, there will be infusions of literary voices as well as other things.

Some of these communities in Canada have very well developed language programs to save their traditional languages or, in some instances, actually to reintroduce them, and often as the first languages. What's your position with regard to such programs?

I think it's good that they are preserving languages, Native languages. For the writer that question is probably less important than it is to, say, the anthropologist or the ethnographer, because the writer is going not to write in the indigenous language, he is going to write in English.

Why?

So he will have an audience, a readership.

You don't envisage that there will actually be a written literature of any extent in any of the indigenous languages, for sheer market reasons?

That's right. I think that's right, that's a fair statement. I don't think so.

This is not a problem that's just arising, nor a problem within the Indian communities only. Isak Dinesen wrote in English—because she wanted to be read. That's what the Navajo writer is confronted with, the same problem. One can write something in Navajo now because we have an orthography for the language, but nobody will read what is written in the Navajo language except someone with a very specialized interest. And writers write for readers, and they want to be read by a large readership—that's one of the goals of a writer, I suppose, in any culture. Writing in an indigenous language does not serve the writer's purpose.

Does that imply, too, that the major relationship that you see is between the writer and his or her audience, rather than between the writer and the group from which he or she emerges?

No, there are both things and it depends, I guess, upon the individual as to which is the more important. Both things serve his purpose, I think. If a writer is Cree, it is in his interest to know the Cree language because that will strengthen his understanding of the oral tradition—that's his ancestral interest in language—and make a better writer of him. But at the same time the better his knowledge of English, the better his writing, too. So both things serve his purpose. The point I was making is that he will not write in Cree, however—though it's useful to him, a knowledge of Cree.

As the technical media at our disposal become more manifold, do you think it is possible for a writer to envisage a sort of double existence, publish in both languages? Some writers in the South Pacific have thought about that, at least. It would raise fascinating questions within the individual writer's mind, regarding translatability.

It would be a good thing, as it was—again to cite the example of Isak Dinesen—as it was not a bad thing that she should write in Danish at all. But had she been limited to writing in Danish, she would not be nearly as well known as she is now.

I have a totally isolated question with which I'd like to finish: the question of violence. (We talked about violence a couple of years ago at one point.) How do you address the question of violence in your work? Do your texts advocate any sort of attitude towards it, a perspective towards violence? It has fascinated me how you were dealing with Billy the Kid, for example, the degree to which you aestheticized violence. It has in a way worried me.

[Laughter—apparently delighted]

So there is the question: Do your works establish a perspective, an attitude towards violence?

I think the answer is probably, yes. I am fascinated by violence, I suppose, because it is a manifestation, in my mind, of evil, and evil is something that is intrinsic in the Indian world, and so I come to that *respect*, honestly.

I also believe that violence defines to some extent the American character. We are violent people, as you know, and we don't seem to be retreating from that, unfortunately. Billy the Kid was a violent man. He lived in a violent time—there is a new book out on the Lincoln County Wars in which the author describes Lincoln, New Mexico: it is a one-street town, it has only one street, and that street was the most dangerous street in America in such and such a period of time. From 1870, say, to 1880 a hundred and four people were murdered on that street. Certainly it is hard to ignore facts of that kind, and I wonder about them, and I am intrigued with violence. And I know most Americans—take the O. J. Simpson business—sat enthralled to watch that damned Ford Bronco with a fleet of police cars behind it.

Do you also establish a link between violence and style? Do you tend to stylize violence? Or are you fascinated with the way in which violence becomes a style of living and is stylized in certain gestures?

Am I intrigued by that? Yes, very definitely. It's a kind of choreography, *can* be, as in the case of Billy the Kid's escape from the Lincoln County Court, I suppose.

And what then? As you represent the stylization, and as you yourself are stylizing the violence through your language, what happens to the violence? What sort of attitude on the reader's part are you anticipating?

That it will be a fascination, that it will incite the imagination. As it does, clearly, if you take Peckinpah's *Pat Garrett and Billy the Kid*. There are moments of violence in that film which are pure choreography, in slow motion, even. And you begin to appreciate that violence can exist within a kind of aesthetic framework, and that there is a design, and there is proportion, and there is symmetry in this violent act. And as a people, Americans, I think, tend to exploit that. That's an aspect that appeals to the imagination.

Isn't this sort of aestheticization of violence almost an endorsement of it?

Yes. Yes, that's the dilemma, that's the problem.

Can your texts then be read as endorsing violence?

If you want to read them in that way, certainly.

[Laughter—from both interviewer and interviewee]

And I suppose every time you do have an act of violence that is described in that artistic way, yes, it is an endorsement. But this violence may be prevalent in the United States. It certainly has precedents in ancient literature as well.

I wouldn't doubt that, but you know, you began by establishing a link between violence and evil. Are we suddenly in the area of, well, Satan being much more fascinating, much more interesting than God?

Well, isn't he? . . . But I think if you consider something like *Beowulf*, for example, Grendel is violent and evil, the two things are indivisible. And this probably is an idea that goes back to the beginnings of history.

All this occurs within texts that are also concerned with the historical violence that has been exerted upon the Indian. . . .

Yes.

Texts that in a way also again and again implicitly, or even explicitly, try to present an indictment of that violence.

So on the one hand you have an impulse towards an indictment of violence—an accusation, basically—and on the other hand, you've got this aestheticization of it, this almost-endorsement of violence. What does one do standing within that tension?

One, I think, appreciates the tension, is enlivened by the tension, is provoked and undergoes a kind of transformation, has a "high," an experience as it were.

But to your question—and I know that you are interested in this question of violence, and so am I. But as it works in the Indian world—trying to go beyond the idea that evil and violence are indivisible and that they exist within the Indian world at the deepest level in terms of witchcraft and so on—but to take it beyond that, if you think about the infliction of evil on the Indian by the white man in, say, the Indian wars, that's an interesting thing to me because the Indian wars followed upon the Civil War, which was one of the most violent conflicts in history—the Battle of Gettysburg, for example, was a bloodbath in a real sense—but there was a kind of nobility in the Civil War. It was a war fought on principle, people were fighting for the preservation of their homeland or for the preservation of the Union, or for the freedom of the slaves. The Indian wars were entirely different. There was no nobility in them. I think they were racist wars. I think the Indians were killed because they were Indians. And it was hard put for the soldier, the cavalry soldier, to look at his image in the mirror and be proud of what he was doing, whereas in the Civil War it was different. And there was a kind of eloquence in the Civil War, on the part even of the infantry who would write home in the most eloquent language about their feelings and so on. The eloquence in the Indian wars fell to the Indian. There are interesting comparisons there.

But the evil, you know, was on the side of the cavalry. The massacres were mostly theirs, and so the Indian has been, in novels and films, a popular victim of evil, and the white man has been the perpetrator of crime, of evil deeds. And the violence of course was rampant, rampant acts of violence.

Do you know, when we talk about violence in American literature or in the experience of the American Indian we are talking about a very complex thing. It's not easy to condense it, put it in two sentences, or a paragraph. It's very complicated and complex.

In moving from House Made of Dawn *to* The Ancient Child, *would you accept the statement as relevant that in* House Made of Dawn *one is more clearly within these various tensions, that there is violence as sheer evil, racist violence, and there is the fascination of violence in the killing of the albino. There are other perspectives, but there is in the killing of the albino the aestheticization, which in an interesting way is also almost a sexualization.*

Yes.

Whereas in The Ancient Child, *it seems to me, there is a more consistent aestheticization, through Grey's fascination with Billy the Kid, through the filter, maybe, of the dime novel.*

I would agree. I think that the violence in *House Made of Dawn* is much more concentrated.

It's also more complex.

And it's, as I think of it, a kind of major consideration in that novel. It may be not quite as major in *The Ancient Child*, but certainly there is the circumcision and so on.

At one point some time ago you said you were interested in the Manson family. Is that interest still alive?

Yes. I've got a novel in the works which is set in California in the '60s and deals largely with memories that I have of that time and place. It was a very interesting period in our century, and the Manson people figure in it because they entered into my life in a peculiar way. I don't know if I ever told you this. When I was at Stanford—this was in the '70s, this was after the '60s—one day I was keeping office hours and a number of students were coming around, and the last one was on her way out and she said, "Oh, Scott, there are a couple of people out here waiting to see you, really interesting people." And I said, "Send them in." And in came Sarah Good and Squeaky Fromme. And they had the X's cut into their foreheads, and their eyes were glazed. They were both very pretty and polite.

And they informed me that Charley Manson, who was then at San Quentin, had sent them to me to ask my permission to live on the land. Somehow through the reading of *The Way to Rainy Mountain* or some such text he had got it into his mind that I was the custodian of the land and he should have my permission to go. And so I granted him permission, graciously, and we had quite a little chat. And a couple of days later I had a call from the FBI in San Franciso, and they said, "Your name is on a list in Charley Manson's possession. We don't know what it means, but we thought you ought to know." And if I hadn't seen the girls before that and known what this was likely to be about, I'd have probably been frightened away, worried about it.

So that stayed in my mind for a long time. Also, Charley—we were in the same area in the '60s and we were about the same age, so I have given him some thought. I am interested in what it is about such people—Billy the Kid is another—who inspired such a loyalty on the part of their people. I don't know how you account for someone like Manson. Billy the Kid I can understand to a greater degree; he seems a likeable guy, a fun-loving kid, and he loved life. Manson, I know, was something else.

And you are trying to find out?

I'm thinking about it, yes. I have even thought of trying to talk to him and to Squeaky again—I don't know whether I'm going to do that.[20]

I got to go.

20. *As of 1997 the novel was being written.*

TWO

Gerald Vizenor

A preliminary remark first: You must have realized there is no strictly linear arrangement to the questions.

There is *not*?

There is not. They circle back to certain things again and again.

Circles? How am I to be able to understand this if it's not linear?

Well, we may want to jump at certain points, back and forth.

But let us start with the first one. Do you find it problematic in any way, in the framework of "appropriation of voice" and all that, that I, as an obviously non-Indian academic, am doing these things?

Not at all, except—you have the signs of wisdom which cause a kind of reverence, when one is in your presence.

Are you going to conduct this in the ironic mode? What does this portend?

It's your very wispy gray hair and your tall and gentle, affable manner that. . . .

It's easy for tall people to be gentle.

That's right. . . . You give it away . . . that's right.

Thomas Wolfe—the 1920s/30s writer, not our contemporary—has something about that. . . .

So you don't find it problematic at all. Would you react differently if you had an Indian interviewer here?

Probably not, but the questions might be different.

In what way?

It's possible, depending upon the place somebody lived and grew up in, and their experience that they want people to ask a playful question arising from some shared experience. That's a possibility, a kind of experience of patois, some playful energy.

Which of course would certainly not be the case with somebody who is not only not Indian but not even American.

Ah, yes.

That would conceivably constitute another barrier.[1]

But we *are* discussing a text. You are the reader and interpreter, and I am the writer. So you know more about it than I do.

Is that true?

Well, there are so many readers, readers, readers. A professional interpreter of the text certainly has multiple interests to study the text rather than just a passive, escape reader. Not that somebody would be reading my work just for escape literature—maybe liberation, but not escape.

So, the questions. . . . First of all I have to embrace the idea that there are no responses appropriate to questions. Questions lead to a kind of discussion, and I'll probably spend a lot of time avoiding questions, and in the course of doing that, we'll talk about it.

Exactly. . . .

Since I can hardly answer[2] . . . I mean, obviously concrete things—"Where do you come from? what do you do?"—linear things, which you just said you are not doing.

No, not really.

But interpreters have. . . . You know, your pursuit of the text is specific and precise, and you are approaching it in an emotional, academic, and intellectual way, and your interpretation is different from mine, of course—I don't even know if I have an interpretation. My rereading of things is to see if I did that right, not if this is working in a larger sense of comparative literature.

In this context of reading and rereading texts, how important are notions of "an Indian literature" to you? How separate, do you think, is such an Indian literature from the rest of literature?

---

1. *Isn't it curious that we should use all manner of playful evasion to evade seriousness, and seriousness to evade playful evasion? What does this imply about situation and topic? What does it imply about the stresses built into both?*

Play is a metaphor, seriousness is positivism.

2. *You were primarily prepared to talk about your work—and ultimately we did obviously talk about it. But had you anticipated a different approach? Or more of an "approach"?*

Questions are playful approaches. Whose questions would you answer?

Obviously the two extremes of that discussion are that only Indian writers can write about Indian experience and. . . .

By extension, only Indian readers. . . .

Yes. [Laughter]

Now, the difficulty with that is, there are those people who have a lot of experience with Native material or people, or whatever, and have an ineffable energy about it, that is, they feel in the presence of it. I can't describe that—that would be the same thing in reading Herman Melville: there is an ineffable energy that's present in a text that some readers are drawn to and some are not. Now, those people are drawn to Native American literature and find its good meaning—and I don't mean the political part of it; I think in fact it may be a handicap if readers are drawn to it for its ideology and politics in order to do, say, the service of some political party or some opposition to American history or something like that—that's a completely different argument. But I am thinking of the story and the play of experience and how we come to it and are touched by it.

Of course there are differences, but are the differences critical or essential? I don't think they are essential. Otherwise a number of writers would never have been able to touch it, and readers would not have so enthusiastically embraced so many books by Native Americans. There is a fault, however, in America and the rest of the world—but I know America best in terms of some of its reading faults—there is a primary fault that texts that are in translation are hardly appreciated as such. I refer specifically to *Black Elk Speaks*: unless someone is alerted or trained or educated about translation, most readers don't think of *Black Elk* as a translated work, much less can they appreciate without some classroom instruction the difficulties of that text getting into print. I mean, the complications of translating a *spoken* language to the printed page.

That text is embraced in a very romantic way, and of course we have in that text the presence of John Neihardt and his daughters, as well as Black Elk and his son. I mean, that's a group text. It's a beautiful book—that isn't the point—but the parts that are insurgent, the sentiments attributed to Neihardt, are the most often quoted by romantic readers. So, you see, the fault here is in this: on one extreme are readers who embrace Native American experience for its romantic interests, the other extreme would be the search for the text that has a political and ideological presence.[3]

How would you react to the suggestion, then, that in a certain way there is an aspect of translation to all Native American writing insofar as it exists between cultures and in many instances between languages? Ultimately, certainly, in all instances between languages, even if the particular writer does not speak the original language of his or her particular group.

As we speak and listen, we translate—not in the same sense of language to other languages, but we certainly do have to translate context, intention, meaning of words, not all the time but most of the time. We couldn't possibly engage in any kind of friendly discourse if we didn't have some positive motivation of translating as we speak and listen: experience, our differences, embracing a kind of understanding in the midst of all that. Do we dare say that's what's happened between Native American cultures and the Western world? Very difficult to embrace that idea. . . . [Laughs]

That's where notions of conflict would certainly have to be put right next to notions of communication, translation, and all that.

I play with the argument that if a Native American text is embraced too warmly, too generously, and is something like a best-seller, there might be something wrong with the interpretation—not necessarily the text, although that's possible too, but there may be something wrong with the interpretation. If the experience seems so acceptable to a mass market by way of interpretation and the general sense of translation, there may be a fault there.[4]

Would that apply more strongly to American Indian literature than to all literature—because in a way you could of course toy with the argument for literature as such, right?

3. *Have we slipped here from one opposition (being "touched" by a text versus using it for political purposes) into another one (romantic versus political), and isn't the former constituted along the line between more or less legitimate reactions to a literary text, and the latter a polarity of (comparative) illegitimacies?*
The opposition is rhetorical.
4. *Can texts protect themselves, or can they be written so as to be protected, against such misinterpretation? Or is the very indeterminacy that you (we) tend to attribute to literary texts a "guarantee" of the possibility of misreading?*
The text always waits for the next reader.

What makes it more extreme a condition of interpretation is that it's from oral to written. There are connections from, say, other European languages, written languages, to American English; of course they are cognate—religious experiences; an embraced world view; monotheism, generally speaking—I mean there are so many shared experiences and traditions, not to mention the immigration over a period of a hundred years, two hundred years. But to embrace in translation in English an oral traditional story from Asia or Africa would have as much a problem of "What is the context?" as does the translation of oral material from Native American creation.

My argument focuses in that respect on the *Trickster of Liberty* stories. I advance that idea there—of course it can be argued [against], but *my* interpretation of trickster stories in oral form is that they are temporal, they only exist in a kind of language game where there are speakers and listeners who are engaging in it; they don't exist otherwise. I mean, they don't exist in a monologue. In other words, it has to work, it has to have some play or regression or extreme that works in some context of speakers and listeners, and that's dynamic. It's not passive, it doesn't function in a passive sense. So it's almost impossible, it seems to me, to translate such a thing without some literary artifice, without some literary style to give the context of that same play. Such simple devices in some way alert a reader to listen, to hear contradictions—and that would be going on anyway—it can't be transcribed and translated so directly, but [is] a kind of stylistic interpretation of that speech and event in the story.

In the background of what you have been talking about is the idea of a good translation, of a proper sort of translation of the type of material that cannot be rendered directly.

An imaginative one, please.

Yes. Are you by any chance familiar with the texts in English by Harry Robinson, the Okanagan oral storyteller?

Don't know him.

It's a fascinating text because it has been published as a sheer transcription. And the marvelous thing is that the transcription throws the reader back on his or her own resources again and again. You can't read it quickly, you can't read through it; it brings you up short because you don't understand the references, and you have to put yourself into an oral situation mentally, imagine the storyteller there behind the transcription. But none of what the storyteller does, implies, etc. is rendered verbally in the text. The reader has to provide that. In a way it does directly the opposite of what you are talking about: where you are trying to put into the text some sort of equivalent of the context, it leaves that out.

There would be differences with Robinson and Kalifornsky, say, the Athabaskan storyteller who wrote in an orthographic system and then that was translated; you have two texts, you have text to text. But what I'm getting at is this: almost all of the trickster stories from the Anishinaabe have been translated already, and so you have just fragments of references to content and circumstance and situation of the stories. We know of course that much of it has been sanitized. It serves the translator's interest of what constitutes the story, the narrative form, and the ethical-moral interests of the storytelling; much of that has been imposed.

So I have very few examples of any traditional texts that were written by a storyteller in either a phonetic or an orthographic system. That makes part of the difference. But even storytellers today in English have the same pattern of play, so you see the same playful presence of these stories. I am less enthusiastic about emphasizing the trickster part of it because it's been embraced in an almost "kitschy" way now, it's become a kind of American "kitsch," the trickster, especially Coyote.[5]

As in Santa Fe.

Yes, and it's spreading rapidly, like killer bees. Coyote-kitsch is almost universal.

My second question was something like, People tend to look at literature in terms of a group literature; they try to establish a relation between group, author, texts—a sort of constitutive, generative, legitimating relation. How happy are you with the idea of a responsibility of the text to a particular group, of the author to a particular group? How necessary is legitimation by a group to you?

---

5. *So the response to the threat of commodification would be evasive change, constant vigilance, and quick reactions? That would make the surface of the text very closely dependent on one's assessment of the present.*

God loves you, upper- and lowercase!

The group we have to work with is Indian, and this is both a tragic and a comic burden. After five hundred years it's comic.

Why?

Because none of us is the victim of Columbus any more. Practically everyone has access to the idea that "Columbus didn't punish me personally," and then we are stuck with this word "Indian," as unsatisfactory as it is, however inappropriate it is historically. But we are stuck with that, and so it's a condition I call "postindian." We all now work and speak, and communicate in playing language *after* the invention of the Indian. So we are "postindian": a postindian language game about who we are after the invention of the Indian by Columbus. But we are stuck with this word "Indian," and the tragic part of it, of course, is that the word has for almost all of its language history been pejorative, or a word of fear, or a word of obstacle; it's been a troublesome, a difficult experience to be touched by that word and to be in its group. But that has changed. It's not to say that there aren't tragic prejudices that affect people's lives by the very word "Indian," but it has changed. America embraces romantically not the *absence* of real people, but the *simulated* spiritual presence of the Indian in a kind of New Age movement.

But to think of literature as Indian literature, just to deconstruct that, is to say, well, that's a literature of invention. I mean, there are no Indians; there are only those people who must by colonial obligation take up in the English language the use of that word, because it's a shorthand for ordinary communication. How difficult it would be throughout our lives if we had to challenge at every instance the use of the word "Indian" and many other words, say, the word "Sioux" or the word "Navajo"—I mean these invented words. That would be a terrible burden, and we would have much less pleasure in communicating and would constantly be at war in language rather than at play in language.

You are addressing this on the level of terms for the group, rather than in more political terms that would refer to the people who form the particular group. Where do they come in? Where do actual people who are being called "Indians" come into the game?

That point. You were speaking about being grouped and literature having a group identity. And the other contradiction is that, of course, if we speak of Indian literature, then we reduce the rich complexities of human experience of every tribal group, of every writer coming from a uniquely, distinctly identifiable experience. If we reduce that by this colonial word, in my view we don't have a literature worth considering except in its political sense or ideological sense. And surely there are people who embrace that. They embrace a literature they can use against America. And Europeans like to do that, too; they like to take up the group literature—"Indian"—and use it against America—the Italians, and Germans, and French take some pleasure in that.[6]

Why, do you think, is that so?

Maybe because there is some envy of the power in the world, of American institutions and products—and just presence, I suppose.[7]

Is it also possible that Europeans, paradoxically in a way, tend to focus more on the internal contradictions within America and also on the discussions within America of the contradictions in America? For example, the critical aspect of Thoreau tends to be focused on more in Europe, by and large, than in America. The subversive Melville seems to be even more of an interest in European criticism than in American criticism.

But neither Thoreau nor Melville are being embraced because of their difference racially and culturally. It is true, of course, that other immigrant groups have been of international use in an anti-American position, but Indians are a perfect universal symbol of victimage.

It may in part be that many countries must bear the contradictions of their own history, especially Germany—the agony and horror of their recent history—and it may be of some comfort to Germans who are tired of bearing that burden to point to America

6. *This comes out as if you had waited for an opportunity to get rid of it. Has it worried you a long time? Because "the Indians" can here once again become a pawn in a game that is not theirs? Can you specify when and why you felt this for the first time(s)?*

Karl May, and the thousands of "Indian" clubs in Germany.

7. *From my perspective, not just envy of a "presence," but fear of active interference. I won't throw the word "imperialism" at you, because it is somewhat late in the game to introduce it, but it is a word that is once again being applied to the relationship between the U.S. and other parts of the world.*

We are talking about the bourgeois simulation of Indians in Europe.

and say, "You have your own record of genocide." Nothing comparable there, but still that may be a motivation.

The other problem—which I don't want to get to right this moment, but a bit later, since we are not going linear here—is the investment in America and, I think, in most of the privileged Western world—not the burdened Western world, but the privileged Western world of leisure economies—the investment in a victim. And I think it's a part of monotheism, and it's where Western civilization has had the most power religiously and economically; there is an investment in the victim. And communications, literature, popular ideas and culture sell great victims, and "Indians" are the simulated universal victims. Victims have no humor; they offer the world nothing but their victimization, and that makes people who invest in them feel better. It's a great emotional experience, they can draw upon it metaphorically, and yet the victim never talks back. When the victim talks back, they stop being victims.

But back to this group thing. The answer is *yes*, ideologically and politically. But let me make this even more complicated: we have thousands of distinct tribal groups before Western settlement in the Americas. But since Western contact it's not only the unique, distinct tribal communities and cultures and languages that become part of contemporary literature in the imagination of the heirs of those cultures and communities, but think of the experiences they have had with different colonial occupations: the tribal groups in the Pacific Northwest, the Athabaskans and various other tribal groups, with the Russians; there were the Spanish, of course, in the Southwest and West, and then Spanish-Mexican[s]; French in the Great Lakes and the East; and English and Dutch and Finnish and Norwegian—and everybody. But the primary colonial impact has been Spanish, French, English, and Russian. That has all had an impact in very unique ways on different tribal communities, and through intermarriage. Many Anishinaabe surnames are French from the fur trade. Some tribal groups had less contact between each other than they did with colonial agents. For instance, is it any surprise that I could say to an interpreter of my work that I have more in common with the French than I do with the Lakota? What would be so surprising about that? It's not politically correct, it's not an ideological advantage, but in terms of imagination and literature and story it is a condition that cannot be ignored.[8]

Does that also imply that you would opt for a radically individualistic approach to works and their authors?

Well, I have never seen or heard about a successful group novel. Works of imagination are not in isolation, I don't mean to suggest that, but let me use a metaphor from tribal experience. It's the vision quest or, properly speaking, the idea of a vision quest—but forget the quest, let me just say that in its most general reference individuals are called upon for whatever reasons, either urged or grudgingly pushed or inspired to seek, some unique connection in their life—meaning to the place, the environment, a time, a culture: a vision, so unique, so unique that no one else in the world has the same vision. Now, that's hardly communal in the Western sense of the word.

It's communally sanctioned.

Yes, that's the difference. It's communally sanctioned because, although it's dangerous—and in fact the person who searches for such a vision may be dangerous to the community—nevertheless, communities look upon such extreme imaginative experiences as having value to the community. Now, that's a bit romantic, there. They are seen as having value, but one also knows that an incomplete vision may be in fact the most dangerous experience, more dangerous than to have no vision at all. Is the writer's work any different?

What would be the equivalent community sanction with regard to a writer's work?

A writer's work—the sanction would be within the powerful motivation to give a good voice by way of an interior vision to the collective experiences of a tribal community.

And who is the community there, for the writer?

For my experience the community is of course a traditional Woodland one, but it's also colonial, it's also the impact of the

8. *Connections and backgrounds are, then, largely given, rather than chosen. Organic metaphors of experience and writing—next to all the equally prominent and valid notions of free play?*
The context is colonialism.

French. A whole story cannot be told without speaking of our heirs and our ancestors and the situational tragic wisdom of our life experience.

Good. The corollary to the whole thing is of course—how universal is literature, or should literature be, in your opinion? On the one hand you've got this community sanction, on the other hand we do have the possibility of translation, going on and on and on, basically embracing the world.

Well, are there human beings that never tell their story?

Probably not.

Probably not. Most people never get their story translated or transcribed. Few people do. But then not everyone chooses this extreme form of the vision: literature, I mean, the writing of literature. And it is an extreme form, no one asked for it, and you have no idea if anybody even wants it, and you may not even know in your own lifetime whether it has some value, apart from your own interest in it. It's a form of madness, it's an extreme interior vision, and I don't know where the voices come from that I hear, but I know it's extreme. And I can sit for hours and months, literally, and not hear it, and then in some unusual way, sometimes in that presence of half-sleep/half-awake, there's a transformational moment of consciousness, when you dare not think too closely because you'll go to consciousness, that events come to me.

As you look at those events later on, how much factual, so-called ethnographic or anthropological knowledge do you think readers need to really get your texts?

Mine personally?

Yours, and maybe also other writers' texts, but primarily yours.

The general response first, that not all writers have to pay attention to the material already published. It certainly would be, I think, important, if an idea is in contradiction, to have some sense of what the contradiction is. So, if for no other reason, it's important to have some sense of the historical material, the ethnographic material that's been published about your community, your tribal group. Not exhaustively, of course, but the general critical ideas that have informed professional communities about who your ancestors were.

Does this also apply to the readers of your books? Do they also have to have. . . .

Well, I was responding generally. Specifically I pay a great deal of attention, but I have to tell you I have an advantage here. Anishinaabe writers have been quite distinguished in the history of published material. I think among all tribal groups in America the Anishinaabe have probably the largest number of writers, going back to George Copway, William Warren, the first historian. There is an advantage there, but an advantage that I must contradict, because it would be fairly difficult to embrace Copway's views. Although what I *can* be deeply moved by in Copway's work—and it gave me access to a much richer vision—is his very simple descriptive story about how he was converted to Christianity. Is that any different than a vision quest? It was a bolt of lightning, and a terror, it was a powerful experience. If I didn't know that story I would have less appreciation for the possibilities of the evangelists in the woods, serving a people who have already a well-established history of receiving inspiration from people's visions—why should they fall so much for the outsider who purports to have a powerful vision?

Now, I am not arguing in favor of fundamentalism, because these were *individual* visions. Their power was sanctioned, of course, but they were powerful individual visions, and the Catholic church I don't think would embrace those visions because they'd be in competition with the interpretation of the priests and would be the work of the devil rather than the work of God. I don't want to get into monotheism, so. . . .

As for my own experience, I make critical use of just about everything I can find that's been written about the Anishinaabe. I don't always put it in my work, but when it's in contradiction, I do, or if it embraces, I do. I don't know of anyone who makes as much use even in fiction of actual ethnographic and historical documents. I don't footnote, but I quote, I cite, and I don't do it out of context: provide the text, the context of when it was written, borrow a quote, sometimes in agreement or disagreement, sometimes in contrast, most of the time in argument, and [I] work that into my own experience—of course that's part of the experience. If I'm defensive about that material, I give it too much power. If I embrace ideas in an argument, I gain power in my own argument.[9]

And what are the implications of this sort of intertextual strategy? What are the implications for the reader? Do you think you're guiding the reader clearly enough with regard to the use of those quotes? Do you provide enough context, or are you really sending the reader to those other things and saying: now go and read a little around what I have used, what I have made of it?

Oh, I can't anticipate what a reader will do, but some readers do that. I don't think you have to. The way in which I use material from historical, ethnographic, and religious sources is to borrow the ideas and work them into an argument or a scene or a situation. For example, a couple of times I've worked around the following incident that was reported by Walter Hoffman on the *midewiwin*. There was a healer in a tent, and they tied him up, and there were a lot of witnesses around, and there was a wager. The local minister was present, and he was very worried about this; of course, extraordinary things happened and they were unexplained. Now, you know very well from Hoffman's point of view in his writing that he did not look upon this as anything other than trickery. The minister present was terrified it was the work of the devil. The Indian Christians who were present wondered about the tricky part here and were quite impressed with it. I placed that *one* situation in the center of a larger story.

But I have never entered any of those things in the consciousness of a character. I don't take up the consciousness and privilege of, say, the trickster, to show that Hoffman is wrong, in that sense. I'll create a fictional situation or I'll report another actual situation to argue with Hoffman in a different way, or of the people who are present that he reported on. That's not such a good example—it's too complicated.

It's OK.

You are much too kind, or are you being ironic?[10]

9. *The anxiety of influence?*
Influence is the least of my worries. My work has a vision. What you might consider influence is a metaphorical footnote.
10. *Neither.*

You have connected your writing very clearly with an Anishinaabe sense of group identity. Now, I was struck by the many interactions that seem to be proliferating between indigenous artists, indigenous writers all over the world like, for example, Canadian Indians cooperating with people from New Zealand, from the South Pacific, etc.—almost as if the notion of the indigene was becoming an internationally available notion, and as if coalitions, indigenous coalitions, were being established all over the world. How do you feel with regard to that sort of development? Is there an international notion of the indigene that makes it possible for indigenous people from different parts of the world to communicate on a different sort of level than they would communicate with nonindigenes?

Clearly, I would embrace the argument that there is in the Americas a sense of identity arising from this, that the colonial experience is enough of a bond, the consequences of colonialism are enough of a bond, to share a kind of common sense of identity and presence, of being the first cultures in a place. We are mixed-bloods now and that's what intrigues me, and fascinates me. It's also the honesty of my own experience, and I would have to challenge almost everyone else that it has to be theirs, too. The notion of something like a pure blood is a Western invention.

So you would actually even within this notion of the indigene be more interested in differences than in samenesses?

That's right. The differences are much greater, and the differences may even be a greater bond, intellectually and imaginatively, than the terminal sense of ideological and political interests. Those are short-run, short-term. And they haven't done very well in the history of the Americas.

I am not arguing integration in a subtle way; that isn't the point. It's that we already are so diverse, so complicated that if we can embrace some common experience with all of that diversity, we have much more intellectual power than the simplicity of an ideological position that we are the victims, that we share this common victim's identity of colonialism.

What would be the common experience that one could embrace?

It would be this diversity, that in fact we are not victims. We have a tragic wisdom that arises from these contradictions. It's not passive, it's dynamic, a survivance energy that gives the Americas its best history, its greater meaning. For instance, William Apess—speak of contradictions—publishes probably one of the first Native autobiographical texts, in 1829. What he is writing about *then*, in 1829, a hundred and seventy years ago, almost, is what America can barely embrace *today*. He says of himself he is Pequod, he speaks of that as a source of his identity, he will not accept the victimization; he speaks critically of oppression, but he says, I am a mixedblood. The idea that there were pure tribal groups is another problem. But here is a person who is speaking directly of this very diversity which he himself represents in his own writing—no, I don't want to say "represents"—he himself imagines in his own writing, something that people can interpret as a more powerful representation of experience than the essentialist position. A person like Apess never disappears in the literature. An essentialist does.

So that you would actually couple the notion of difference, of embracing difference, notions of fluidity and dynamics, with the notion of survival. And then you would ground survival not in the preservation of this or that essence but clearly in change, in dynamics, in the ability to deal with history.

I think one advantage is the diversity of tribal cultures, and of mixedbloods. The diversities of these experiences are not reduced by nationalism. The advantage, I think, that Native Americans have is that they are the indigenous populations, the first cultures on these continents. That's enough to have both a factual historical and a romantic connection. I mean that it isn't enough just to say "here first," it's to say "of the land." Everything after that is our diversity in this colonial sense. But it isn't reduced by nationalism. American Indians embrace the diversity of other Native Americans in the Americas, and so do they elsewhere.

You rejected your own term "to represent" just now.

Because representation has to be textual. People don't assert themselves representationally because representation is determined by an interpreter. And it's a very difficult idea that I argue against. Representation too often serves dominance, as it has for Native Americans. Colonial dominance. Once represented in a written language, by description, by methodologies of the social sciences, by established fields of knowledge, the Native becomes the object and the eternal victim. I've been trying to get out of that. But that's part of our challenge, too, isn't it? Overthrowing the methodologies.

I think we have dealt with that question of stability and change—you are definitely on the side of change, as far as identity in history is concerned.

I am not.

You are not. . . . OK. [Both laugh]

It's chance, though, I argue; it isn't *just* change. It's choice and it's chance. It's not predetermined and it's not essential.

In this context: You've got a language to work with, you've got a culture to move in, that are both full of ethnic stereotypes. How should one deal with these as an indigenous writer?

Well, I have a number of devices in my stories, but to change language, to change words, one must be a postindian crossblood.

Does "to change" here imply "to purify"?

No, it means to reduce the power of the previous word. In time, of course, there is the chance that a word like "crossbloods" would bear different but equal difficulties. But then we'll come up with another word. The representation is not in the language. If there is any useful representation, it's in the dynamic exchange of ideas which are more imaginative in situations that serve people, rather than in serving methodologies and lexicons and the people who issue these words, the institutions of dominance.

You are reverting to notions of power. How does one work against established power? What sort of power does one need oneself? What sort of authority does one need oneself? How does one prevent oneself from basically falling into the same traps of power that the dominant language has again and again fallen into?

I'll have to begin with something even more naive in a way.[11] You have to live in a constitutional democracy to begin with, and I don't mean that lightly. I mean that it is our good fortune, by chance, and in spite of the horrors of colonial domination, to bear the consciousness of a constitutional democracy. I am not being idealistic about this, but it makes it more possible and thereby less politically difficult—less politically difficult doesn't mean it isn't

11. *Ouch!*

92

difficult—less politically difficult in the fundamental sense that I would not be killed for my ideas, and it would be difficult to lock me up or forbid me to speak and write.

One possible counterargument that one might hear in this sort of discussion is, Isn't the very fact that in most Western countries one is so free to dissent an indication that the dissent doesn't ultimately change the power game in those countries?

But it certainly has changed the game. I'm not embracing casinos right now because I think they will end up being the ruin of many communities—that's my personal argument—but I have to tell you that the prevailing view everywhere is that this is a chance that communities have never had before. That they are making money that they never would have had a chance at in any other way. That's extraordinary.

Where else in the world could Native communities turn treaties and contracts with governments around to benefit them in that way? That's extraordinary. It hasn't been easy, and it's far less than anything anyone would accept as a good settlement, but here we are. We have a situation to deal with at the moment. We bring together our intelligence in the best way we can, and our good sense of politics. And it is quite extraordinary that each generation has developed a body of knowledge, imagination, and tragic wisdom to argue in court the sovereignty that Native Americans knew was intrinsic and obvious.

In this context, how would you react to the argument that there is something radically wrong about any kind of democracy in which the actual participation in the political process as evidenced by the number of voters, for example, falls below 70, 40, 30 percent?

Even more dangerous, of course, are the lobby interests. Probably you'd have to say that the only way you'd have something functioning in an ideal way, as a representational government, is when there is no economic interest, so you don't have any lobby interests. And of course that's preposterous.

I also find it very worrying—and not just in the States—that the number of disaffected people seems to be greater than the number of people who are participating in the political process.

Well, it functions in the judicial system, and the judiciary is a separate branch of government. The executive or president can still function shrewdly in political terms. That can go wrong, of course, as it has so often, but at the same time an executive bears some ideals of his time.

Does that mean that you see progress—because you do see progress of sorts—that you see progress happening within those areas that are dominated by the educated elite?

The best and the brightest are seldom so in government, but in spite of the economic interests, and the lobby interests, the election of the government still attracts many people—and not just through parties—who are serious about serving the community and a constitutional democracy. It still is a form of representation that attracts idealism—and disillusionment, but it still attracts generation after generation of idealists. And also, established political families maintain their power in government service. Some of that power is public service, an uncommon idealism.

Should we fault, for instance, the political interests and traditions of the Kennedy family? Of course, government service is always an argument, but should we fault a dedication to liberal issues? We can argue, but we can't fault their idealism to serve disadvantaged populations. The Kennedy family has done more than any other family in politics to serve the needs of Native American communities. They initiated legislation in education, public health, and other concerns of poor families on reservations. An argument, of course, but not a fault of dedication and service.

So the interesting thing would be that it is oligarchy and a type of aristocracy that are seeing to it that democracy works?

Europeans might notice that, but I don't think you can say. that a democracy works that way. Certain families, who may or may not be aristocratic in their politics, do carry out the historical ideals of a democracy, as so many other families and organizations that are not suspected of being aristocrats.

Or they make up for the faults of the actual democratic process?

They may, yes. Who has the leisure to anticipate that there could be so many faults in a system of government? Yes, the so-called Founding Fathers. Some could be seen as aristocrats, some not. They argued and established a constitutional democracy, one that favored a strong federal government, which in turn would better serve the interests of Native Americans. I mean, would the individual states, the more private interests in those states, have established treaties with Native American communities?

How do you react as a writer to the question of art and exploitation? Do contemporary artists exploit in their writing the cultural heritage of groups within which many individuals are mentally or physically starving? It has something to do with the general question of academic knowledge and exploitation. How do you react? How would you tackle the question?

I have always encouraged Native Americans to be their own artists, to write (as my interests are in writing). The American Indian Literature and Critical Studies Series of the University of Oklahoma Press encourages young writers, and the idea is to use Native American material in a new and original way, that is, our situations of meaning, with a new vision. And in this way we have already published first novels by young Native Americans who might, *might,* have some difficulty finding a New York publisher. They are not recognized as Indian writers. In other words, they don't write in a way that New York editors are familiar with— meaning the popular romance of who are Indians. I said earlier in our interview that I am suspicious of books that are too popular, out of New York publishers, because it suggests something about the misinterpretation of a popular culture, or misrepresentation in the view of the popular culture.

So, to answer your question, the way I pursue this is to bring as many Native American writers into print [as possible] with all their diversity, their power of imagination, and it renders, slowly but surely it renders all of that romantic work and exploitative work boring.

What you cannot then abolish, though, is the gap between those that do have the ability to produce work that will get published and, to use a romantic term, the mute masses.

Yes. Oh, we are made all the stronger by the fake. We need the fake. We must have the play of the fake to remember who we are and the best imagination of our time.

A related question: On what does one base one's authority as an artist? What is the source of that authority, of that legitimation for your own utterance?

My own vision. I have no authority and I am illegitimate as an artist.

Well, unless you say, of course, that that stance precisely is one that legitimizes whatever you say.

I didn't mean to get caught in my own binaries. . . . [Laughter]

How would you write or tell the story of Indian writing in North America? Where are the beginnings? What are the major phases? What's the importance of '68–69? What's the importance maybe of House Made of Dawn? *People have talked about* House Made of Dawn *as a sort of germinal work.*

I would have to separate the incredibly rich complexities of *House Made of Dawn*—what a great book!—I would have to separate that discussion from the prize recognition of the work, because the prize served something else, not the powerful complexities of that work.

That was a great act of imagination. Momaday has certainly given us the contemporary voice that has a kind of courage to speak with complexity and diversity. The prize, however, did something else. It brought attention to what was thought to have been a nonexistent literature. But you can't fault that either; I mean, people didn't even know there was a literature before that, so if now they discovered there was, it's not a fault, it is an opening. The first critical study in Native American fiction followed closely after, by Charles Larson, *American Indian Fiction*. That was the early '70s, just a couple of years later. I'm quite sure that this national, indeed international, enthusiasm for Native American contemporary literature two or three years following the prize— longer than that, but a very powerful initial enthusiasm for this undiscovered literature—was like a new colonialism.[12]

Now, consider this *new* literature. So many works were published in a few years after *House Made of Dawn*, but isn't it an irony that the first serious critical study of Native American fiction is, about that time, a book like *American Indian Fiction*, a badly faulted work. He used social science methodologies to interpret a rich and powerful imaginative literature, and it has a lot of envy in it, but not a whole lot of good sense about imagination. So that of course

12. *So you are again profoundly ambivalent about the recognition, the reception of a Native work. Which raises the question whether recognition is at all possible without some degree of misprision, doesn't it?*
Ambivalence is a precise condition of Native American literature.

the next book published was ten times better; I mean, no matter what it was, it was better. But that was a beginning also, of critical writing on Native American literature. In a way it had never been approached before. It always was approached as the cultural business of the social sciences, and had never really been approached seriously as literature by a literary scholar. Unfortunately, Charles Larson touched on that in his methodologies.[13]

Do you see any consistencies and dominant tendencies in the representation of non-Indian people in Indian writing?

Well, the weakest representations are the binary racial structures. I only allow certain characters in my work to use the word "white" because that's as much an invention as "Indian." Maybe we could say there is the "postwhite" as well, or postcolonial is the postwhite. But some writers actively engage in this very familiar and popular binary racial contest. I try to avoid that; it's, I think, too easy a hit. The sources that give meaning to that binary are so complex and so diverse that it seems to me anyone worth their measure as a literary artist must try to establish characterization and situation and complexities that would give meaning to an expression, not just throw the structure of White and Indian at a reader. Even though readers recognize it readily and quickly, and embrace it.

In that context, to refer to another binary pattern: Some of my students have been worried by the representation of women in quite a few Native American texts, finding them chauvinist to a certain extent. Do you have any reactions?

Well, I don't. It depends. If it's in characterization, do we hold an author to fault for the representation of a reader? Doesn't the text have its own reality? And should texts be written through some template of politically correct sensitive thoughts for the moment? If, however, it's a strong narrative voice, or if it's in the first person and the author is so present in that first-person voice, or is a very strong narrative voice making editorial comments that don't necessarily give good meaning to the story, probably it is a good point to make.

13. *So that Larson should be read as a transitional figure, rather than a true innovator?*

Not at all. He practices the worst of social science rubbish in literature.

I think in many instances this has had something to do with the statistical evidence, too: fewer female characters who manage to master their lives than male characters, fewer female characters of any great complexity than male characters. I think it's this sort of charge. More dumb women than dumb men.

I think they are right. [Silence]

"I think they are right." [Both laugh]

I don't think I want to cite the authors, I'm just quickly thinking of my own responsibilities as a writer, and I don't set out to make heroes or heroines of my characters, but I certainly have a wide range of very complex characters who have great power, and they are men and women.

More men than women?

I should hope so. I'm a man.

Ah. I think that aspect probably does come in—that there are more male writers out there.[14]

Do you find that Indian writing is characterized by writerly strategies that clearly differentiate it from non-Indian writing? Is there a sort of Indian voice that comes through in the writing?

Well, Indian writers make. . . . It's reaching for these group ideas that is difficult. . . .

I'll try it a different way: In much of what I read in Native American literature the authors make active and immediate use of mythic material that's associated with traditional experience. Now that doesn't mean that's what the truth is or that's what's essentially a property of identity. It does mean that authors who write about Native American experience make active use of these sources of past experience. I do. I also make very active use of published documents. Another experience I find in Native American literature is the connection to environment, but that's not as strong, in my view as a reader, as myth. Then in some cases it's almost passive as if the environment is essentially pure, true, and honest. Again, my view is that the landscape, the place is dangerous—*that* to me is more of a traditional sense of

---

14. *And one could follow this up. . . .*

The woman in me writes differently than the man the reader encounters as the author. My gender must be implied by the reader.

environment than taking up the kind of Western romance of the environment as pristine and beautiful and a reservoir of hope and resurrection.

Mother Earth.

Now, Momaday does not do that. Momaday establishes this significance of the source of inspiration in characters' relationship to landscape. He doesn't make it a safe place or a Mother Earth, but he makes it a powerful source of imagination and mystery in a character. But often writers will just fall back, as they do on the binary of race; they'll fall back on Mother Earth as a great provider, and how dare we? . . . And that sort of thing. And I consider that more of a weakness than a fault. It appeals to popular culture. To me it's not a great literary inspiration.

In this context people refer again and again to the oral tradition, and that's probably a valid comment in view of what you have said earlier.

I was going to reach for that next because that's one of the ideas, along with myth, that's probably the most frequently cited in the discourse about what's different in works by Native American writers. And I would say that in this reference to the oral voice or the presence of an oral tradition of some kind, there are so many contradictions and difficulties, in this kind of language. *Oral tradition*—oral is anything but traditional, it's foundational, it's what all human beings do, and even some animals. If it's *tradition* in the sense that we all make sounds and our primary source of identity and connection to each other is through sound, and that our brains function primarily through giving meaning to sound in the ear and not image in the eye, we have something to talk about. Now, I think that Native American writers quite often play to the power of oral experience rather than traditional experience. And they do it in a number of ways that are not uncommon to any writer, or many writers. There is a lively dialogue that sets up a communal situation rather than, say, just one powerful protagonist's narrative voice like a charger—a lively, even contradictory, dialogue or discussion between characters. A leap of memory that goes to past conversations—not past texts or literature, not literature, but past conversations—and dreams, to visions in an oral performance.

What I'm interested in, and what I find in some authors, most notably Momaday—I also find it in Luther Standing Bear and Jim

Barnes, Louis Owens, Louise Erdrich in a more complex way—I'll
come back and touch on that—what I am interested in as a writer,
and what I find appealing to me as a reader with a sense of
imagination, is trying to discover this mystery of an oral memory
or voice in writing. I mean it can't *happen*: here's a text that has no
connections to anything, you know; there is nothing under the
printed page. And we have to say after all these years of this post-
author time now, too, we can't hold the text to an author's biography. So we have some real difficulties here as Native American
writers, as we mature individually and as a group, you know,
identified as Native American writers—we have to mature with
this, we have to realize that just because we have the tribal connection by way of our ancestors [it] does not make the text
essential or authoritative.

What we have to find here, and that's what I have been
working on in *Manifest Manners* and elsewhere, is to find a new
critical language to interpret what is a Native American text
without depending just upon proof of the author's identity. We
need something much more sophisticated and intellectually
powerful as a way of interpreting a text to say this has something
in it, it has the power of a place, of a culture, of a time, of a voice,
of an oral memory. If we can do that, then we don't have to worry
about who is Indian and who isn't. Then we have a powerful text
that we can interpret. And should someone come along who has
no ancestors who were Native American but has the power of
imagination to be present anyway—all the more beautiful is this
imaginative work.

What is it then? Well, we can't hear the text except in our own
interior voice. Now, should we have exacerbated the problem
here? An Indian reader reads differently than a white reader? I
don't know. I don't think so. Of course people interpret memories
differently, but how different are these memories? Do people reach
back into a great distant dream of tribal presence before colonial
contact? Or do we all reach back into a kind of common emotional
life of sound?

*Weren't you in a way positing, on the one hand, the single indi-
vidual and, on the other hand, a set of universals, the universal issue?
And aren't you sort of setting literature up within that tension without*

referring to an intermediate set of culturally, historically guaranteed conventions, conventions of speaking, perceiving, writing?

Seeing, maybe. I'm reaching here for an idea I call "shadows in the word."

Anything Jungian in there?

No, that's a different kind of shadow, that's the universal archetype. Those are good thoughts, but they are monotheistic.

This theoretical problem of author and implied author is something that's really interesting in our discussion right now.[15] Does a reader imply an author? Of course. Who knows the author? Very few readers know the author, so they imply an author. When I read Momaday, I imply the author and I know Momaday. I mean I read because I have heard him speak, I hear his voice sometimes, I hear the power of this visual description in his voice, and I also have an implied author: a person of great mystery, someone, especially in *House Made of Dawn*, on a dangerous vision. I don't mean he's dangerous. I mean that encountering the unknown is dangerous, and there is that edge, that shadow of the danger of human identity in that implied author's voice.

Are you using the term "shadow" here with any implied reference to The Ancient Child?

Yes. Medicine bundles are shadows.

Then there is the implied reader. For whom does the author write? If the reader has the theoretical privilege of discussing by way of interpretation two authors, the real author with the biography and the implied author, that raises interesting questions about markets. Whom does New York promote? They promote the implied author, that is the author who is the romantic Indian. And it's best if they have physical features that satisfy this implied author's romance. Jamake Highwater would be a perfect example. He was more beautifully and romantically Indian, the perfect implied author to satisfy everyone's New Age fantasies of access to the secrets, the interests, the power of Native American experience through literature. He was probably the most successful

15. *Do we need to say here that this will return to the question of "shadows"? Or have I just said it?*

The shadows are the presence not the absence. Shadows are the silence of oral performance. Shadows are the implied contradictions of literature.

implied Native American author that ever lived, and he should be honored in some way.

The absolute fake is an important experience. It teaches us something: If we are so significant, why is it so easy to fake it? Well, of course, it's easy to fake it because of the incredible investment in the simulations of Indians. And the simulations have become more important and more significant in America, in the world, than have "real" people and their experiences. That's not a new idea, but it's a critical one in terms of Native American literature because it strengthens the implied author more than it does the biographical author. If publishers were to look at the complexities of every Native American author they might not publish them. All Native American authors are mixedblood. They all have very diverse and complex experiences. Not one author would satisfy even the minimal requirements of the implied romantic author.

And now the implied reader: We have the author's idea of a reader, although I have to say I don't write to a reader. I write to somebody I think is listening, in a kind of language game with me; and I don't mean that I'm tricking somebody, I mean it's the play in the shadows and richness of language and it's more than a discussion, it's a dream discussion. I'm in charge of the dream, and I can prompt people how to speak with me in this dream. Where is the reader for that? There are some listeners, but I don't know where the readers are. So I have difficulty with this idea of readers, but I don't have any difficulty with implied readers. I don't have a reader in mind, but I do know what implied readers are; I know that there are certain readers who'll have more pleasure with my work than others. That's an implied reader. University students probably, because I do make use of a lot of ideas from history and literature and linguistics.

And you refer to places like those outside the window.

Exactly. Where people would have some experience by either reading or travel. I also have an implied reader who is Native American, and that's a strong implied reader, too, because I make also references to places, times, and events and situations that are obscure to every other reader. I don't intend them to be obscure, but I am not going to apologize for the fact that somebody doesn't know enough about that.

And you are not worried about the different readings those different readers would give to your text?

I don't know how to worry about that without weakening my work or appealing to popular cultural demands. I don't know how to do that. So I may be demanding in those terms and I accept that responsibility and perhaps that fault, too.

Which is a nice way of obliquely addressing the question of elitism.

[Laughs] So we have all these complexities going on in the text, and I think we are finally freeing ourselves as a collection of very complicated authors, who are simply congregated as a group to represent something that sounds like nationalism, in other words a national identity of writers. Those categories are necessary to present groups of books, but they are giving way. . . .

Somewhere in here I have the term "poly-traditional." I think you have also implicitly referred to the fact that contemporary Native American writing to your mind definitely is poly-traditional and very wide-ranging.

Yes. Many readers, many voices, many authors.

Now, "shadows" I didn't get to, and what I have been writing on is this:

I use the simple illustration of the name Luther Standing Bear. He borrowed his father's nickname when he went to boarding school as a surname; it's not *his* nickname.

[Tape change]

Luther Standing Bear. . . .

I was talking about Luther Standing Bear, whose last name is a nickname of his father, and then at the Carlisle Indian School in Pennsylvania, he was asked to choose a name among hundreds of first names, and he chose "Luther." And in his writing he speaks of this, of his father's name, his father's nickname, and he tells of how his father was so courageous and *earned* the nickname Standing Bear, meaning he "stands to fight" as a bear would, and does not yield. Tremendous courage.

The point I'm making is that the shadows, or the shadow stories, surrounding the name "Standing Bear" are what give it meaning. Now, as a writer, I try to reach for the shadow. I don't know all the shadows, but I do know some. How do I come by some shadows? I come by them from my own family experience, from my own imagination, from reading, from encounters and experiences and excitement I have had with human beings, tribal and otherwise, everywhere.

So "shadow" always refers to something historical rather than something universal. Historical and specific. . . .

I would say "specific," rather than "historical."

I'm using "historical" because one needs to distinguish this kind of shadow also from the timelessness of the archetype.

Now, any reader looking upon the name "Luther Standing Bear" in the context of a Native American Lakota storyteller, of whatever kind, any reader can give that meaning. The first meaning they'll give to it in a popular way is that this is Indian, because that's a descriptive name, Standing Bear. Any reader, even people who have been to the zoos and nowhere else, will know a bear is big and tough, and Standing Bear—they might easily, in a very popular way, think of the name Standing Bear as powerful, even in the context of a zoo.

Those are limited shadow stories, about the meaning of that name. Other people will look upon "Luther" and think, "Hah, isn't that interesting, an Indian has the name 'Luther,'" and think of the Reformation or whatever—another different source of shadows. I doubt that anyone who knows the story of Luther Standing Bear would ever think of the Reformation; they would think of the Carlisle, Pennsylvania, Indian School and a choice of arbitrary names from which to choose one—it could have just as well been Charles—he didn't know actually what any of these names meant, or even how they came into the English language.[16]

Now, "Standing Bear" is more complicated. If you know the shadow of the story behind his name, every time you read the name you are in touch with the shadow story about that experience. How rich and complex can that be! Let me even make it popular in another dimension, though, rather than specific: Let's

16. *You are right about the moment of choice, of course. But what about those "shadows" one can imagine the name to have acquired for Luther Standing Bear himself as he later learned about its origins? Shadows of rebelliousness and complicity, of idealism and venality. . . . What of the possible play of attraction and rejection, between the self and its name?*

Shadows, in this sense, are political. Names and shadows in literature are *not* the romance of primitivism and innocence.

say a Native American is reading this. Do they read it like a zoo story, Standing Bear? Never. Any Native American in a Woodland tribe or a mountain tribe, any Native American who has been around bears—and I can't imagine a Native American who has not been at least very close to bear *stories* in one way or another—but anyone who has been in bear stories, heard them and been present with bears, lived with them in some sense by way of imagination or in the flesh, gives that story a completely different meaning. And so would, of course, some other person who has lived among bears; but if you are a Native American it takes on a special shadow dimension because of the power of animal totems in the myths and beliefs of tribal stories.

So, I'm working on this idea of shadows; I use that name only as the simplest example. But let me try to expand it a bit and say, "Isn't it possible that most situations and character development by way of imagination or experience would have rich layers of shadow stories that are accessible to the readers in different ways?" Now, this kind of an interpretation creates a more complex and powerful reader. It is not just implied reader, popular culture reader, or other implied readers. Readers who are not Native American can have access to very rich, powerful, and complex shadows that enrich a story.[17]

Which means that different sets of culturally determined and personally determined associations would legitimately be filtered into various kinds of readings of the same texts, would produce those various readings.

Yes, a shadow story.

God loves you. Do you know that?

That is a shadow story? [Pause] Tell the shadow story.

[Laughs] Well, the shadow stories would be dreams—and how do we come by dreams?

---

17. *We are in the area of notions of associations of ideas, of ambiguity and ambivalence—of a multiplicity of meanings that in some sense adheres to the text: its richness makes for the richness of the experience of it, or the multiplicity of readings is in some manner centered in the text (rather than being, centrifugally, the result of differences among acts of reading). Or, to put it differently, differences come together in mutual association and interconnection, rather than warring with one another or canceling each other out. Difference is associated with communication?*
God loves you.

What an incredible mystery, what an enriched shadow story I am in now! And they are independent, they have no representational source. Literature has potential to be equally as powerful, and Momaday is among the most powerful. His *Names, House Made of Dawn, The Way to Rainy Mountain.* . . .

I won't ask you what you think of the development—this is going to go out of the manuscript[18]—I won't ask you what you think of the development from House Made of Dawn *to* The Ancient Child*—because I myself am not sure what to think yet. Only I found that, upon a second reading,* The Ancient Child *is much more powerful even than at the first reading, and that has given me pause.*

It's much more precisely controlled.

It's extremely consciously written.

I have had the unenviable task of writing a short review of a German translation, and the thing does not translate at all well. It was a bad translation, but I also think this book is much more difficult to translate than the earlier ones. Much more difficult.

Now, this question of Western traditions, Western genres—I mean it seems to me that in Native American writing there is a pronounced tendency—and you have just referred to The Names, *you have just referred to* The Way to Rainy Mountain*—there is a pronounced tendency to violate decorum, to transgress the borderlines between genres. And all of your writing is one single transgression of this sort. Why do you think is this so? And I'm asking less for your personal reasons in writing your own things than for your analysis of the situation as a whole—but clearly, since you are one of the major transgressors, your own experience would go into this interpretation.*

Maybe it's possible because I never took seriously any courses in writing.

Ah, but that raises masses of questions about the influence of creative writing courses on the development of indigenous writing all over the world.

Yes. It can be seen and felt.

It can be seen and felt everywhere.

Yes, that's right.

18. *Why should it?*
Continue in the shadows.

So we have a second line of argument there as well.

Now, there are powerful stories within those recognizable forms that arise from influences and writing schools—Iowa and elsewhere. Within any style are powerful experiences and shadows. The form and the style doesn't necessarily deliver the power and the imagination. I think most styles are restrictive and the best storytellers I have ever known have no recognizable style.

Would that refer to the Native American framework or to writing in general? I'm after the question in a way whether postcolonial writing or indigenous writing would not have more of a tendency to move outside of the established patterns in order, maybe, to create a sense of cultural difference.

Well, I think it's appealing to consider the ideological tension here: if you are already marginal, then why not perform a marginal style or form? I suppose you could advance that argument as a conservative[19] explanation of the surreal and avant-garde, but there are other ways to discuss than the political and ideological one. One would be within literary interpretation and the theme itself, and clearly the extremes in expression and story are what give us meaning. You know, it's the extreme presentation of experience and ideas that gives meaning.

And in my own case now, if you look upon the standard popular cultural presentation of tribal people and literature, I must reach for the extremes. There is no meaning in what I see, so I must reach for the extremes. And it's more than that. It's not only reaching for the extremes of style, it's also finding ways to overturn, in familiar and unfamiliar ways, the very content of popular ideas about Native Americans. That I must say is the easiest to do: being in a position to controvert (and I am not talking about revising, but just overturning, controverting or exposing the weaknesses of . . .) is the easiest and sometimes the most delightful part of what I do in writing. The most difficult is to find the underlying vision and shadow, to give some power to the character that's not merely a cartoon surface contradiction, binary, or *just* overturning.

That ties in nicely with a problem some of my students have with some of your texts. We read Wordarrows *last semester, and with some of*

19. *Why "conservative"?*
Causal reason.

107

the stories they felt that basically it did not leave them with anything to hold on to, that you had been so skillfully setting up and then deconstructing all available positions that there was nothing ultimately left in their hands except for the problem that it had all been about. But your phrases just now implied that you are not only after deconstructing things, you are also after. . . .

Transformation.

. . . Constructing images of—of what precisely? You used the term "character" just now, but it's not a character's essence that you are after. It is. . . . If we take the term "character" and this notion of shadows together—could one say that it is character as experience, once again in time?

Yes. But I'm after the reader's soul.

Oh, what does that mean?

That means—nothing. [Laughs]

Go on. It was such a nice sentence.

Well, Nathalie Sarraute argued and then wrote a demonstration of her idea of *tropisms,* the idea that a reader must be prepared for the experience of the character—I'm oversimplifying a very subtle and brilliant idea that she developed and demonstrated in her literature and in her book called *Tropisms.* With that in mind, the easiest way to attract a reader to the contradictions are the well-established binaries of popular myths and ideas about Indians—they are so well established, you don't have to work very hard: a feather, a tipi, the Iron Horse—I mean, you know, it is everywhere—Mother Earth, the Great Spirit, it's everywhere.

Longfellow did it for us. *Hiawatha* is the foundation of American consciousness. So it's an easy task for any writer and, I must say, pleasurable, on a superficial level it's pleasurable, to set up these kinds of contradictions for these obvious expectations the reader comes with, even though many readers don't want necessarily to fulfill those expectations. I'm not faulting their interests in literature, I'm just faulting the popular cultural presence of these things. So it's easy to contradict that—but not enough, of course. So what I'm after is that [if] you get a reader engaged in the easy disruption, you have created a kind of political tropism. The reader is engaged in an instability of familiar references or tropes that may have given the reader meaning before. Now, to just go to the confrontation or the difference is too complicated. Readers will not accept it. But you can set it up with some play of duplicity and contradiction—it does act to a certain extent—and again I am borrowing a really wonderful idea from Sarraute that it's set up as a kind of tropism, this play. Now, most readers and storytellers and people who listen to stories do recognize this pattern. It's a sort of fencing, a kind of contradictory play of binary exposure, an engagement in the opposites, a subtle recognizable play of extremes. No commitment yet. He does not have to be committed, he just has to be overturned. It does, I think, at least create the possibility, and my intention would be to do that, that they are now ready to appreciate—more than they would have before they read this—a much richer and more mysterious and contradictory presence of a character who has his own doubts and cannot perform according to the expectations of a popular cultural image of a Native American, and may not even know his own sources of imagination. Some of the characters in *Wordarrows* do have this power, a kind of mystery that they can't articulate in their own way. Let me think of Laurel Hole in the Day, a fictional name for a real person. By the way, the difference about *Wordarrows*, compared to my other writing, is that the only fictional aspects in that book are the ways in which their stories are told and their names are changed. All of those stories came out of the tragic wisdom of human beings I know and who struggled to gain some meaning to a difficult moment in their lives.

And one of the fascinating things about the book is that, on the one hand, you have got all this postmodern play with language and, on the other hand, you do have, you clearly indicate, the documentary aspect. That tension works marvelously.

Laurel Hole in the Day did come in, and she couldn't speak. I knew that; I have seen that in hundreds and hundreds of people, even in myself at different times, that if you spoke you would come apart with rage, with pity—you dare not speak, there are certain moments one dares not to speak. Not because you are going to insult someone—not that at all—it's not a social burden. This is an interior mystery, that the burdens are so great that, if you speak in a culture that will fail to understand one more time, you cannot survive. So the inactive survivance in her case—and it's not uncommon, there is nothing uncommon about any of those characters, although many readers would think so. My shadow experience in these stories is that there is nothing uncommon. Laurel Hole in the Day might have disintegrated and lost her power of survivance. What a rich and imaginative person! I knew this power; it's of me, too. (Not because I'm Indian. But that's important to that story. It wouldn't have worked otherwise.) I said, *write* it then, and she did.

I did that once before with a non-Indian person. I was a social worker in a prison—a story I have yet to write; it's a big and powerful story. It's the only saint in a Western sense of monotheism, the only saint I believe I have ever met, and he was committed to a prison for carnal knowledge. He had a massive speech hesitation, or a stutter, and he was judged to be mentally deficient because no one could understand him, no judge, no authority, because they never took the time. I mean, nobody could understand him, so they judged him mentally incompetent, deficient, and sentenced him to prison. The person he had sex with was a woman he was in love with. They were in love with each other.

He was one of my first cases when I went to work as a social worker in a prison, and they gave this case to me because I was the new guy, and this was trouble, difficult. And there was a kind of prestige of cases, right. This was a troublesome case. We talked for several days, and I could barely get one word out of a hundred, I could barely get a context for things, I tried to go for yes's and no's. He was a loving man and I felt that. I felt he was wronged—that was my instinct, those were the shadows I even sensed in the stutter. And finally I had this insight, and he was stuttering away once again, and I said, "Ben, whisper." When he whispered he didn't stutter, because of course he didn't voice anything. So then he told me the story.

Well, my point is that he had the other extreme. He was trying to tell everything—past his survivance, the truth of his own experience—and it just tumbled over everything, he just couldn't be heard, whereas Laurel Hole in the Day knew that through one more word she was past survivance, and she wrote it out. What a powerful person!

Here we have classified you as a postmodernist, and what you have just given me, in associating the notion of character with a notion of mystery and with the notion of a language that tries to get at the mystery by indirection, is thoroughly modernist.

No, shit. . . .[Laughter]

It just proves that there is no rigid borderline between those things.

But what you have also said, I think, is that, however much we may be moving in language, and however much we may be constituted by language, we are not constituted by language on one single level. . . .

No, never.

. . . But there are depths beneath the surfaces of language, and it's precisely this that modernism has always been after.

Well, to say that there are shadows beneath the words is modernist.

It is.

Let me add this point, so that you understand that I don't avoid these contradictions, I actually embrace them. I am a modernist by way of the appreciation of the imagination of characters, and especially those characters with whom I have had a real experience and whom I have tried to present in fiction. Clearly that's more powerful than modernism, that's survivance. Now, in fiction, characters of course arise from people I know, sometimes composites, everywhere. But when it comes to the racial binaries I am a postmodernist. When it comes to historicism. . . .

Then you perceive postmodernism as a strategy. . . .

That's right, absolutely. The trick is to be historical in a world of postmodern survivance.

As an ultimately political strategy?

I would say a strategy of interpretation and literature, yes—it has political power, of course, but it's hard with television. . . . If I were writing in the '20s and '30s, that would probably be about the last moment of political power in fiction. Salman Rushdie, we all know, of course, but his are the consequences of religious power, not political power. But it's hard to imagine, with television and communications in America and most of Europe, that literature has the kind of political power it once might have had.

That gets us into a totally different area, the way the academy, particularly in America but also elsewhere, has established itself, in its own mind, as a place of high political importance.

And it's not.

Or inflated out of size.

I have seen much more power politically in the voice, or in the absence of the voice of Laurel Hole in the Day, than I have seen at universities. . . .

[Pause]

That was a pretty nice way to get modernism and post-modernism in. But see, the other thing. . . .

It's also a nice way of using the distinction and subverting it as a simple historical sequence.

One doesn't serve all.

I wouldn't use modernism to explain or to interpret that experience, but I would prefer to come up with something implicit in the Native American experience: a theoretical approach to interpret that. On my own side, the problem with modernism is that you bring with it of course traditional values of mythic interpretation, you truly do, out of Western literature, so that makes it. . . . The method of interpretation is present, but the source of cultural experience that gives that method meaning is the difficult part for me.[20] And that's where I have to reach to overturning the modern, overturning the establishment of what represents a text and experience. If I were to go modernist, then we would have to say something universal about Laurel Hole in the Day. The universal would diminish what is implicit in that experience.

You referred to the avant-gardes etc. earlier on, and it's that side of modernism, too, that I am interested in: the search for alternatives to a dominant culture. And once you've got that in your notion of modernism, then I think you can establish the relation with Native American writers as well, because I think the twentieth century has been characterized by a search for alternatives to the dominant culture.

20. *Is one of the problems you have with modernism, its primitivist tendency, too?*
Yes, the nostalgia for the primitive.

One of the things I've argued, and it's playful, is that Native Americans were the very first postmodernist artists in their stories. Clearly a story was not representational, not even the origin stories that people think were something equivalent of liturgy—anything but that. The origin stories had tremendous variations depending upon the circumstances, the people present, the storyteller, his or her abilities, and then every serious, so-called *serious* origin story had the tricky, playful origin story as a counterpart. And no story was ever the same. Of course not. The story is in the ear, not in the text. The story is not representational.

Can I add this question that I have somewhere later on? Do you see any danger in using terms like "modern," "modernist," "postmodern," "postmodernist" in dealing with Native American writing? To do so seems to categorize once again; it seems to subsume the Native American enterprise, the Native American writer, the various texts under those dominant strategies, the dominant terms, the dominant categories in a universalized Western history.

It does, but I select interpreters and critical ideas—I do that in discourse, I mean. I speak of different ideas, mostly from the French, but also from American critical thought. It's important to do that, to show what the enterprise has been and how it doesn't fit or suit the unique and implicit experience in literature of Native Americans. In some cases it is suitable, in others it's not.

I fault the methodologies of the social sciences. Now, it's not the *interest* of that, because that hasn't always been, say, evil or dominant or whatever. The idealists are searching for a way to explain and study and come to national attention. But the reduction of experience, the searching for the generalization that *represents* the truth, must invalidate everything unique in Native American culture. So I *have* to constantly work at that and argue against that; it's not just anthropology, it's not just sociology, it in fact is monotheism as a foundational organization of thinking and world view that's presented in a secular way in the generalizations of something that becomes "the truth."

The connection between monotheism and the academic enterprise being the notion of singleness of truth?

Yes, and redemption, and something *after* this. . . .

Transcendence.

Yes. This idea that we can—like a transitive verb—we can get past this; it's more than the action, and it's more than a moment, and there is a truth, a faux truth.

I've been struck by the frequency of the term "to fault" in your discourse. Would you say that you predominantly operate out of an antagonistic spirit? Would you in your writing regard yourself as a satirist?

No.

I know what it is—others speak of that. I take great pleasure in some stories of satire, but let me show you the complications and contradictions.

I have a powerful voice of place and environment, of season and transitions and changes. Practically everything I've written begins with some sense of seasonal change.

Maybe I could again call on Sarraute. I set the season. I must write that—if you live in a place where seasons are critical, for life and death, *and* stories, *and* visions, *and* travel, everything—it's an important part of experience every day. And it's the one very simple trope that you can use to set the imaginative moment, much like a haiku poem.

That's fine, but then at some point you proceed to judge. There is a pronouncedly judgmental attitude, or at least, there is an invitation to the reader to go through acts of judgment again and again. And isn't this precisely what satire as a genre (again and again) does? Not necessarily offering simple judgments—there are types of satire of course that push you into a very restricted position, but there are others; Melville, once again, comes to mind. Melville in Typee, for example, is very much of a satirist, but a satirist of several different things. One of them is the missionaries, and another one of them is the brutality of what he regards as savage life, and one of them is the naivete of the Western observer of this life. The reader is placed within this struggle of positions and positionings.

Your discussion is very challenging, and as there are subtleties and differences in interpretations of modernist and postmodernist discourse and theory, there is a difference in the sense of satire in Western literature and in, say, the stories or familiar experiences of *some* Native American communities. Let me choose the pleasure of these trickster stories, which may be more easily identified as satirical or ironic.

Well, satire, it seems to me—there is a built-in contradiction here—depends upon a well-established referent, signifier, representation. This is also part of comic theory, that comedy is not easily perceived if the situation and the characters are not immediately recognized. So you need a communal pleasure here. Practically the obligation for something comic is communal, whereas tragedy can be an isolated hero working against the gods. Comedy depends upon this communal sense of something recognizable, not only the communal sense within the story or play or image, but within the reader, the listener, the viewer. Even an oral story, a trickster story, let's say, contains in written form information on how it might have been told, on style and context—is it satire that a trickster story avoids all representation? What I'm getting at is to problematize the idea of satire.

I, of course, write within the ordinary interpretations of satire, and some that are unique as well, and some that are contradictory, satirical/comic. Much of it is communal. Pure satire is hardly ever communal; satire is associated most often with representations that might be closer to heroic, to thematic, than communal play or whatever—because, actually, the idea of satire would be weakened by trickster play. It is again the problem of the play within the text, and then the reader or the viewer or the witness at a theater, or something like that.

Now, a trickster story is not satiric in the conventional sense, because the very precision and humor of a trickster story is the avoidance of representation. It doesn't derive its pleasure or anxiety or comedy from overturning a representation directly. That's something characterized in writing, and that's often how trickster stories end up being recognizable *in printed form*. Verbs are set up like that. Language is binary. It's natural on the printed page to do that, and I do that, but then I also reach for more complexity after that, almost always, and end up with a character where you don't quite know where you are. There isn't much representation left if it's a trickster story.

What I'm trying to do is, get on the page what I think was a powerful literary form or expression in oral performance, in oral communal form, and as soon as some listener in a trickster story would lean toward representation, the story would turn transformational. Again, satire is not transformation. It can be, you can play that, but you can only play transformation if you hold on to something that's being departed from, something representational, or something established: right or wrong, good or evil, something established. The trickster story has no establishment, has no formula of reality, and has no categorical recognition of the real. The story has its own signified in its own telling and transformation, creates its own significance, and it also is communal, again. It's not in isolation on the page.

I choose the seasons in part, I choose the historical reference, I create a time and place that's recognizable. (And then I just completely overturn it.) You don't have to do that in an oral story where people are present, because they all know where they are and what time of day it is and what season it is, as they listen to another season. There are many seasons on the printed page, as many as the readers. The trickster creates the season in some action. Trickster stories start immediately in the action; they don't give the reader, the listener, much motivation.

Well, in a way that's a lot like the way most of us communicate when we are telling about things we have done and people we know, whatever. We don't spend six sentences creating a motivation for a character. You don't have to, when people are present and you are talking—that's taken for granted. Someone might say, "And who was that again?" And then you add something. But in a trickster story everybody knows the transformational figure of a story like that; you don't have to establish motivation. But on the page you must do something, not necessarily motivation, but something that establishes the presence of a character, the stories, the people present, some situation of the seasons.

Now, the other feature about trickster stories is that they of course don't end, there's no closure. It isn't that they just don't end deliberately, right, which is an ending. It's that you don't have to end a trickster story. A trickster starts in some action. Then there are incredible transformations: [it] depends upon the moment, who's present, what you want to do to it, whether somebody walks by (I mean, put them in, too), whatever. Transformation. In every good trickster story I have heard and read, Trickster amounts to shit, nothing, and literally, in some cases, shit. How extraordinary! What a brilliant insight! And I can't pretend for the minute to accept anything of the Western interpretation that this is a developmentally inferior literature, in other words, that this kind of story is how stories begin, and then you grow up and become a novelist. Nothing like that. The reason I can't say that is because the trickster story has such power in it and it's consistent.

What you've been talking about has reminded me somewhat of discussions of Menippean satire. Menippean satire as a sort of—depending which way you look at it—final development of satire or origin of satire, where basically what you have is a multiplicity of representations, and through that multiplicity a reflection on the arbitrariness, the inconclusiveness, of any given representation of life itself. So that as the text establishes more and more orderings of reality, it denies the very ability....

That's right.

. . . of language, culture, etc. to order reality. And the interesting thing is that Bakhtin has actually fooled around with the idea of Menippea, and then after Bakhtin people have recovered certain of the central works that have always been problematic, like Moby-Dick *etc., as in essence Menippean satire. The curious "cetology" chapters that we have in there, the beginning of the novel with more or less arbitrarily selected texts from a library, and all of that, are just catalogues of attempts to order reality, one after the other.*

And in a way, I think what you've been talking about has been also this impulse in your own story to establish something and to point out its limited validity. In part, clearly, this happens through a multiplication of patterns of ordering in the story itself. You have several characters, for example, and such characters establish different orderings....

Yes, but the trickster is no Alice in Wonderland.

And none of them are ultimately endorsed by the story.

And no closure.

No closure, absolutely no closure.

Trickster stories: the trickster amounts to nothing—there is, in other words, no temptation to the heroic (some translators have abused that, but . . .)—because it amounts to nothing, it's not that it is antipolitical, it's just the politics of the story itself. You could argue of course that the appearance of what is apolitical is a terribly powerful interest of carrying out other interests, agendas; but that's intriguing: you don't have the self-conscious authorial closure which suggests political privilege. Here the character—I mean, imagine if much of American literature ended up with a character that amounts to nothing. A better America.

There's some of that in the canonized texts. Take the ending of Huck Finn: *heading out for the Territories, he doesn't want to master anything.*

That's right, but there is the closure of direction.

Now, the interesting thing would be to raise the question, Were trickster stories the same before Western contact? Dare we say that trickster stories may be an early sophisticated literature of survivance? I don't think so, but it's a good question.

Subversion. . . .

The pressure on transformational characters would have been so great, and the influence to resist that already was very strong among missionaries. The trickster was the proof, in the eyes of missionaries, that the tribes were pagan. Many of the stories were translated as heroic moral tales. Of course they disappeared from the stories very quickly. Which brings up, by the way, part of why I often play relationships between animals and humans. You know my simple response is, Why is it natural in myth and not as a love relationship? Isn't that the same? What's wrong with loving an animal? Just the sex?

Seems to be.

In connection with this question of not accepting closure, not presenting anything, any kind of stance, I'd like to go to the question of violence: violence in your texts, violence in Native American texts, violence also in Scott Momaday's texts. I asked him specifically about the · question of aestheticization of violence in his texts, which is very strong, I should say.

Let me start with the most general question: Do your texts really not advocate a stance towards violence, or is violence ultimately the one thing that is excepted from the no-closure axiom?

Violence in a text is an understatement of representation. Take the data, read a morning paper, and tell me if there is anything more violent in my stories. So the encounters and descriptions of violent events, especially in *Bearheart* but also in many other places, are an understatement of an overdramatized and overrepresented experience of Western civilization. It's an understatement of what's happened to Native American communities as well. But I don't purchase any of that; that isn't what's in my writing. That's the response partly to your question.

I don't *intend* to aestheticize violence. I don't think so.

I don't think that applies to you very much. Let me once again. . . . My students at Berne were interesting in that respect—they were somewhat worried about the White Hawk stories towards the end. The question that emerged was maybe, "Is there any notion of justice left in those stories?" Or, "What happens to notions of justice?"

What did they read on White Hawk? In the *Wordarrows*?

It was Wordarrows, *the last section there. The question arose because what your story does there in part is account for the violence that happened in so many different ways that one ultimately asks oneself whether one is left with any kind of attitude towards it, whether one's left with any possible way of acting against or with regard to violence.*

Well, I don't know how to answer that. There is one thing that did come to mind right away, though. It occurs to me that someone in Europe reading this wouldn't know that I had written extensively and factually about the White Hawk case and had published that before.

Now, that shouldn't obligate any reader, but it just occurred to me as you brought that up, that of course I was writing within a community where White Hawk was well known because of my doing; he was in fact pretty well known regionally and in America, through that early work I did. But I'm going to take that point even about the factual work I did, because I think it might hold, although there you can easily read through the documents and the court transcripts that I selected. Maybe a similar problem would arise in a reader there: Where the hell is the author? Where are the moral and ethical values?

Not only "Where the hell is the author?" but "Where the hell am I supposed to be?"

A witness. We all are.

Juana Maria Rodrigues, a graduate student, did an outstanding paper on the authorial presence, the authorial presence in this initial writing on White Hawk. She did it in a small seminar

I taught.[21] I was astounded at the insight. What she said was that, of course, the author is not present, but by not being present, he is all the more powerfully present, not in those stories in *Wordarrows* but in the original writing, which has been reprinted in *Crossbloods*. Juana was absolutely right. When I wrote "White Hawk," I was engaged in that for a couple of years. I was an advocate against capital punishment; that was my interest.

So I interviewed, I don't know, sixty, seventy people connected with the case: family, everybody, anybody who knew White Hawk in the slightest, including teachers who only knew him for a year or so. And I still have half a dozen boxes of notes and material and research, which, of course, I've never done anything with. I only wrote on that case, but when I started writing it, I struggled with style and form, and I finally decided to write myself out of the whole thing, even though of course I was the person who raised the issue, did the writing, organized the committee, got the lawyer. . . . I mean, I was the principal player in bringing this case to the attention of the nation, and got a lot of international attention at the time, especially in northern Europe.

But I had to write myself out because it would draw too much attention to me, and the issue was capital punishment, and I didn't want to be faulted, nor did I want the issue to be faulted, because my ego would be served by the story. And also it's a life-and-death story, and I just didn't want this innuendo to even subtly circulate that I was advancing myself on somebody's life or death. So I deliberately kept myself out of the thing.

Juana, of course, analyzed the text very carefully and found those situations and used Foucaultian ideas, and it was a very, very good interpretation. Now, those two stories that are in *Wordarrows* were two stories that I could not tell factually, so I had to fictionalize them.

That doesn't help your students, because the text has to stand on its own, and the question that they raised is the same question. . . .

21. *Has it by any chance been published by now?*
Yes, in *Genre*, Winter 1992.

The question ultimately is also the question whether you are not in a way writing about a situation, or constructing (in writing) a situation, in which it has become impossible to operate with simple or single notions of justice.

Oh yes. That's what I wrote about in all the factual pieces on that. The contradictions in this case were so overwhelming: an overprotective self-appointed guardian—an orphan—violence in his family—attended a privileged boarding school, comes back, aspires to be a medical doctor, has a relationship with an Episcopal minister—and that's one of the stories—and his wife: it's just everyone playing at the edges of this great young man, the Lakota warrior. And what he was, was a murderer. But he doesn't speak of the crime; he has not articulated a memory of this. And he did very bizarre things that take it completely out of, say, homicide and robbery or carnal violence.

What do the stories then tell us with regard to this very bizarre case?

How bizarre it was.

They leave us with a riddle.

No, they leave you with the point that there is no obvious cause and effect, or form of punishment.

So what course of action do these texts recommend?

They don't recommend any; they are not advocacy. Those two pieces are not advocacy. The fictional work was advocacy against capital punishment, but by the time I wrote those two stories in *Wordarrows*, his death sentence had already been commuted to life imprisonment. No story should depend on that, but the other difference is, though, that in *Wordarrows*, you know, the persona of Clement Beaulieu is set up so that I can move in and out of all of these diverse stories.

Let me rephrase the question: If they don't recommend a course of action in this simple sense, surely any text expects a reader to position him or herself with regard to what he or she reads. What sort of position is the reader's with regard to Thomas White Hawk?

Well, not to Thomas White Hawk, not to Thomas White Hawk. To the people who are his interpreters and keepers.

But he is there at the center, too.

Well, he has already committed his crime. Now the others are revealing *their* crimes.

OK, but if you write a story around a murder, the reader cannot but prevent him or herself from positioning him or herself with regard to that murderer as well.

Yes.

And that's where my students got worried. They didn't have great problems dealing with all the other characters around him, but they felt that he was there, and maybe they even felt that in a sense he was aestheticized. He was there at the center as almost a black hole, with the story not telling them what to think about him. And this, incidentally, while the story itself does become satirical. . . .

Oh yes, intentionally. . . .

With regard to several of those surrounding characters.

Those are trickster stories, and they are satirical because they arise from real situations. . . .

What about the black hole there, which is then the center of violence in the story in a sense?

That's a well-told story then, because we don't know. . . .

OK, then I have to come back to my earlier suggestion, I think, which is that you are leaving that as an enigma, that you are leaving that piece of violence as an enigmatic center to the story. And isn't that to aestheticize violence ultimately, in a curious way?

Well, it could.

You make it fascinating, too.

First of all, again the context is that *Wordarrows* is put together with a persona, and I haven't done that before in any book, but I did that because, again, I didn't want to be the first person, so I created another. And then somebody can fault the character who is the first person.

But there *was* no explanation to White Hawk. There *was* no explanation to this crime. There was no trial. You are quite right, it *is* a black hole. He still has not confessed to it, although he has—he has, he hasn't—he still has not spoken of it. He doesn't give it a narrative meaning—and that in some twenty-five years. I saw him two years ago. He still doesn't speak of the crime as *his* responsibility. He still, in a way, shifts the responsibility, speaks of injustice and how he should be paroled. This is an elusive and difficult case, and everyone around it could not understand the crime. Those people needed this bright young man, needed their bright Indian;

that's what my stories are about. So much of the Native world is unnameable. Violence, silence, and the unnameable.

So there wasn't a center, and the center is not even violence. But there probably is some difficulty in not having a case resolved, because cases of violence do demand closure. There is a story here, but no closure.

Because violence is in a sense an ultimate problem, it cries out for some closure.

In this context: there was his accomplice. . . .

William Stands. . . .

Who was acquitted?

He was acquitted on homicide and found guilty of grand larceny. He'd left the house quite early, and the question was, Was it before or after the death of the man? In any case, he was acquitted.

Because in connection with all these questions, my students pointed out quite rightly that you were describing, in this little area there that was concerned with him—a few paragraphs, at most—you discuss that conclusively in terms of a game between prosecution and defense.

That was the only trial. You see, White Hawk was never tried, and people forget that. And I do say that, there never was a trial. This was very unusual, I think unconstitutional, that the district trial judge accepted the plea of guilty in a capital case—that someone says, "Yes, I did it," and you say, "You did"—because judges don't accept a plea in a capital case. You have to argue innocence, or at least with a full confession the sentence is not death. But all the power was with this judge, and of course that's changed by constitutional requirements now, so that couldn't happen in the same way.

White Hawk was never tried. He had a couple of hearings, one in federal court and one before the parole board, which were the. . . . We had to exhaust the appeals process before we could appeal to the governor. So there never was a trial. The only *trial* was for William Stands, and that's how White Hawk got to be known, so that's where the transcript comes from. Otherwise there would be no public transcript of those proceedings, the confession and death sentence.

And there, too, in a way, the problem of violence seems to vanish: into the verbal game, into the verbal conflict.

It does in court hearings and trials.

Exactly. That's the way I tried to deal with it then. It is part of the very peculiar judicial system which operates with a neutral judge and two parties that act out that conflict.

A competition for the facts. It is a verbal contest for a documented narrative, according to the rules of evidence.

Yes, hopefully. You do not represent it, though, as a competition for the facts. You represent it purely as a struggle of skills.

Oh, indeed it was. Because Stands had an Indian lawyer. He was lucky. It reminds me in a very small way of O. J. Simpson's lawyers. He was one of the most successful criminal lawyers in South Dakota, an Indian, Ramon Roubideaux. White people went to him after they killed their wives because they knew he could argue, he'd win in court. He was very much admired as a trial lawyer.

Which is one of the things that, to my students' minds, is somewhat problematic.

Different kind of judicial system.

Yes, and once again the question is, Where does justice get off in that kind of judicial system?

Well, justice is in the right of the review.

Yes.

In a right for the accused. . . .

It's procedural. . . .

In multiple contradictions and procedures of evidence, rules of evidence.

Sure . . . but that's very difficult to understand. It's a rather different system.

All you have to do is read Camus' *The Stranger* and you have a very powerful representation of the differences in legal reasoning.

In this context. . . .

Violence.

It's violence and language, and what you might call the disappearance of the reality of violence into language. So many texts written by Native American authors deal with themes that one could also deal with in terms of economics, politics, sociology, whatever: alienation, conditions of life on the reservation or in urban ghettos, etc. Clearly it's not necessarily the task of literature to deal with them in those terms, but literature being as prominent—not necessarily as powerful—but as prominent as it has been these last decades, is there a danger of what you might call "culturalizing" these problems, in the sense that in the public mind they appear more as cultural problems than as political, economic, sociological ones?

Well, I don't think I sentimentalize the cultural problems.[22]

Let's talk about *Bearheart*. Here we have a failure of an economic system, and the oversimplified question in that story is this:

First of all, it has a mythical and a historically thematic reversal, a grand satirical reversal, and this is satire because it's history that is established here—a Western expansion encountering the savage. *Now* we have, some five hundred years later, the end of that civilization which depended exclusively on petroleum, and now we have Native Americans moving south, encountering the white savages, the people who had it and now don't know what to do, now that they have nothing. That's a thematic reversal. It sets up a constant historical tension, from beginning to wherever it goes. Politically and economically the country has failed. The oversimplified question is: the country has abandoned all other institutional affiliations and sources of solace, is completely dependent upon an immediate situational and gratifying economic system and resources, and something as easy or as simple as a shortage of gasoline throws the country completely at its violent mercies. It has no other institutions to return to, but a kind of fundamental savagism, which was always a part of Western civilization.

So here we have this complete breakdown. And it reaches to the sanctuaries on reservations. Once again, the federal government in cooperation, within this novel, with the tribal government needs the timber, because it has no other resources. That's very political and economic. In the middle of this are a group of people who are trying to figure out a way to survive. One thing they have to do is move. Well, they are thrown out of this center, of multiple generations, in the cedar (overstated sacred reference, right), they are driven out, and it's their episodes and experiences on their way to a southwestern transformation.

22. *Did you hear that sort of charge in my wording? Here—or earlier?*
No, but the way you characterize the critique of your students suggests as much.

But aren't you precisely talking in terms of culture rather than specific economics, specific politics?

Oil is pretty specific. Petroleum is pretty specific.

So it is. Let me establish another frame of reference for the question.

Quite right, their survivance depends upon a vision of themselves in cultural terms.

A vision and. . . .

And those who fail at it. . .

turning to a different "economy" in the sense of "way of life." . . .

Yes.

. . . rather than to specific economic principles—like the switch from hunter-gatherer to agriculture etc.

[Laughter]

In this sense I think we are still talking culture. I mean, part of the background to the question is also whether you would agree that, in the current intellectual climate here, social conflict is being talked about primarily in terms of culture and ethnicity rather than in terms of class, or "politics" in that sense. . . .

Yes.

And doesn't literature fit into this sort of distribution?

I would say that as to the contemporary arguments here, you are quite right, but I wouldn't say "culture," I would say "race." And that *is* the culture, but it is a racial binary that informs most of the serious arguments. Class is. . . .

It's a no-no term.

Yes. It may explain far more than any other discourse. Maybe that's the risk.

I think that is the risk.

Also there isn't much of an audience for class. We talk about poverty in different terms than you do—and even in a new discourse. We can't depend upon race, the racial binaries of savagism, so we must pay more attention to the common struggles, poverty, things we have in common with other poor people.

Let me come back to the earlier story. It isn't culture in a representational way; rather, there are new acts of survivance. The test of imagination to prevail, not to accept terminal creeds, that's the whole theme of it. Petroleum is one of the economic terminal beliefs.

Yes.

But there is a lot of technology throughout, a lot of dependence here and there, even as an active survivor, on the remains and ruins of technology: a postal truck, this faker in a petroleum yard, or the bankers and breeders who have put together a kind of fascist intersection in Oklahoma, and they test people's terminal belief in things, and if you are that dumb . . . you know, the rest of the stories in *Bearheart*.

There is the word "hospital," here is a political interest in trying to discover the problems through language, rather than through a complete breakdown of social interaction, social responsibility.

So in a way what you are also saying then, I guess, is that there is a text that is as political and as specific about politics and economics as a literary text can be.

Unless I named a corporation, I can't imagine it could be more specific.

Now I also think *The Heirs of Columbus* is very political and economic, even to the extent that they wanted to create a new nation to solve the terrible problems in the ruins of the first five hundred years, and they employ—you know they don't do things so much differently; they just have a different vision—they employ modern technology; but they employ it for healing, not for control. Those are contradictions. It is possible to make good use of technology if it benefits ordinary people, but it doesn't happen because its more profitable not to.

I'll have to think about my phrasing of these questions. . . .

The *vision* is cultural.

It certainly is, and it seems to me that even these texts tend to fit into the general distribution that we have talked about, culturalizing versus the class view. But the distinctions must be sharpened.

Well, I am. . . .

Violence is the extreme, but there is no violence in a story unless you think that a text represents violence. There is the description of violence. . . .

There is the theme of violence, again and again. . . .

I do not write thematically.

You can't avoid that.

I write descriptively—an important distinction about the representations of violence. I have encounters, I have characterization;

that's not a theme. The theme, if there is one, is Western civilization: a theme of violence. The readers, not the writers, are thematic.

Marleen American Horse.

Yes.

Isn't there a theme, a very clearly developed theme of violence that she has endured, that she feels she has endured, and that she has to react to differently than she has been taught to react—somewhere in the background of the entire story.

Good question, but I can't answer it in that form, because I have to ask you to consider the consequences of focusing on that kind of violence, *thematic* violence, that creates victims in a story, and all of my writing is against victimage from the very beginning. I do not write about the victim. I write about survivance.

Yes.

Marleen American Horse has endured horrible things, but her whole story, however complicated or innocent—and it's based on a real person—is survivance. She gave *me* courage; she called *me* there. I helped her; she gave *me* courage.

Maybe this is just a terminological problem: Would you accept the rephrasing that that story is precisely about the fact of violence and the necessity of avoiding victimization?

Yes.

In this sense it seems to me that violence and how to react to it is a pervasive theme of yours. It seems to me one can't talk about your works without talking about the fact of violence and the fact that history has been full of violence.

Yes.

But you are demanding, of your characters and of your authorial voices and of your readers, to position themselves differently with regard to violence.

Yes. They are not victims. What I reach for is the tragic wisdom of adversity, not the victimage, and that's the least of what we get in Western literature about Native Americans. We get an indulgence, a sentimental and romantic indulgence in the poor victim. And that satisfies a Western conscience.

Because it establishes a hierarchy.

Yes, it does, and it also aestheticizes the consequences of historical violence. It mitigates the responsibilities for violence, it creates the survivor as an object, and all of that is in the production of one's own sentiments and good feelings.

. . . . [Tape change]

I don't know about you, but I am well nigh exhausted.

I just got started. [Laughter]

Oh, you are one of those terrible people with indefatigable energy?

So we were talking about *not* themes, but characterization of survivance rather than victimage. And I choose the word "survivance" deliberately, not "survival." I consider survival to be a reaction, a response. But if we have *dominance*—in other words, a condition that's recognizable as a world view—then surely we have *survivance*, we have a condition of not being a victim. Now that's exactly what we have among Native Americans. In America they have suffered mightily, they continue to suffer of poverty, of rural reservations and urban. . . .

. . . reservations?[23]

. . . Reservations—they have extraordinary tragic wisdom which I try to write about—and survivance, a sense of survivance. Now, I'm interested in writing about the stories of tragic wisdom in survivance rather than victimage, but again, *popular* literature and culture favor the confessions of the victim, not the strength and imagination, for the most part, of the survivance of these communities.

So, I'm trying to do a couple of things here in my literature. Of my implied readers—I am writing to Native Americans as implied readers and saying, "This is survivance; we must reject victimization and victimry, or not be the object of Western interpretations as a victim. That only perpetuates dominance and objectivism. I mean we are the object of their great insight, and now they've discovered we are victims, how lucky we are!" To the other implied readers, I'm saying, "You are a pack of hypocrites, and here's the violence that you've perpetuated, and here are some graphic examples, and out of this comes tragic wisdom, not your favorite

23. *An interesting moment: the author did not automatically use his own metaphor; I—impressionable reader—did. Is there the question in the background of certain metaphors being more legitimate in one context (poetic, let's say) than in another (an interview, let's say)? And is there a feeling on his part that such metaphors, too, very easily become clichés, so that one has to use them sparingly?*

objective victim. The violence is to yourself as much as it is to the objects of colonialism."

You have several times used the word "tragic." Do I remember correctly that in certain places in your writings—and I can't specify them at this point—you reject notions of tragedy?

Precisely because they are based on binary views?

Yes, I do. In favor of the comic, which is communal. But I do that in the context of interpretation. If we are to interpret cultures you can't impose the Aristotelian description of tragedy as a literary practice. I understand, though, if we were talking only Aristotelian, and if we had the context of his interpretation of what constitutes tragedy, it would be literary, not life. It's people in a position of being a witness to a play, and the play satisfying their pleasure in a thematic structure. That isn't what's happened, though. That literary theme, a brilliant insight stated very simply, has become a kind of world view of monotheism, where life itself is tragic, right? Now, that's how it's used in description of Indians. Life is not that. But if we were just speaking about Aristotle's views of tragedy, there would be a different argument here, or a different discussion.

If you must choose the tragic, I must choose the comic. And this theoretical context *you*[24] are suggesting is [that of] the hero who survives the violence of colonialism. If you must do that, comic theory works better because the experiences are communal. There is no isolated hero; you have imposed the hero when, in fact, the experiences were communal.

But that doesn't hold up here, because I'm saying "tragic wisdom," and that's an idea that Nietzsche considers. And what he is speaking of is that the loss of myth is the loss of a kind of solace in one's stories, which grows out of personal experience and the wisdom of tragic experience. I'm interpreting and making use of this metaphor of tragic wisdom from Nietzsche to say that the manifest manners of colonialism, a form of dominance, invite victimry

24. *Who is this "you"? Who is being addressed? To me, this is one of several nice instances of the different backgrounds of the two interlocutors (as referred to in the beginning of the interview) in fact making a difference: they make it easier for the Native American to address an imagined white reader, because there is a real one present.*

rather than the stories of a tragic wisdom. In other words, here are people whose voice is one of survivance among themselves—good humor, play, and tragic wisdom in spite of adversity—but we seldom hear that. What do we hear? The long suffering, the trail of tears, the victimry, because this satisfies the pleasures of a Western audience.

You could say about the literature that celebrates the heroic that, indeed, this is something Aristotelian and tragic. But when you shift that and impose that as a kind of theme to interpret the life experience of real people, rendering them silent, and objects, no longer alive to tell their own story and to express their own tragic wisdom—in other words, when the manifest manners of colonialism extend to abolish the experiences of human beings— we *now* must contradict the favorite pastime of audiences who take pleasure in this tragic victimization. It's not to say that life wasn't cruel, miserable, and millions of people died—they did— but that doesn't make us victims, that makes us people with stories of survivance.[25]

Does the notion of "tragic wisdom" there also imply a degree of irony?

Yes. [Pause]

I think that way you could, if you wished, get back to Aristotle even, with "tragic irony" and things like that.

But let me tell the irony of violence in this way, then: Shortly after *Bearheart* was published, a friend who was teaching a class at a community college in Minneapolis had assigned *Bearheart* without out reading it—she trusted me—and then, while the students are reading it, she's reading it and realizes this is not a good idea. [Laughs] She called and told me what had happened. We are good friends, and she said, "You have to come and speak to them. I cannot do this." And I thought, "I'm not going to do that. I wrote

25. *So we make literature, or develop a literary perspective, out of the rejection of the application of another literary perspective to people's lives—and the rejection of it as "merely literary." Or, we are moving inside a dialectic of life and literature that needs to remain dynamic, rather than "freezing" humans in this or that position or posture. We are, in other words, once again in the area of the stereotype, but now it is the mega-stereotype of a thought pattern that embodies a world view and creates an entire mode of literature.*

The tragic mode in literature is a power mode of modernism.

it; I'm not going to talk about it." But because she was a friend, I had to do that. I went to the class and, literally, could feel the heat coming out of the classroom. I could have found that classroom without instructions or directions. There might have been—I don't know—thirty to fifty people there, mostly women, many Native American women, a small number of men. They were older because they were coming back to school; this was sort of a reentry education program. If I say older, they might have been five to ten years older than the average college students.

There were angry faces looking at me.

And I said, "Before you ask any questions, let me ask you one: Is there anything in *Bearheart* that is more violent than you have read in your daily newspaper?" Now that took a little edge off it. The students thought about that, and the anger diminished. They understood that newspapers take pleasure in violence. So I had a point established. Newspaper stories are not as graphic and descriptive, but that was my exact *power*, and that's the irony, that fact in itself. So we talked, and by the end I think I had a class of really good readers, and I said things like this: I didn't invent or imagine violence; it's everywhere, and it always has been, and you know it too. It's all over the reservation, it's all over the city, and you know it too. And the worst of it is not described. Why not? Well, because we live in a nation, and a culture, that is ashamed of violence, and disguises even death. We live in a culture of violence as entertainment, a culture that mitigates its own acts of violence. We have limited possibilities to experience the violence that is a complicated and difficult part of our life experience. We are denied the tragic wisdom of the violence we must endure. Our violence becomes entertainment, but not tragic wisdom.

We must endure?

We cannot avoid the experience, the denial, or the entertainment.

Does that imply that the basic reaction or positioning that your texts demand of the reader is realization?

Yes. If we don't. . . .

Well, my point was this: We are perfect victims; in such a culture, the dominant culture, we are rendered perfect victims of intimidation if we don't understand and live with the realities of our own violence. We can be intimidated by the mere suggestion of violence, and that is a form of political control.

The question that arises in my mind there is, Is realization the end?

No, no. Of course not. It's not the end of violence. . . .

No, I don't mean the end of violence. But I mean, Is realization all that is required?

No, no.

Isn't realization, being an aim in itself, also a means to another end?

I think an enormous amount of violence takes place in Western civilization because it is aestheticized and disguised.

Or mechanized, for example?

Mechanized, or celebrated in political ways, in communism or whatever.

For instance, a few years ago, a point that established my argument in a small way, an important way, was in a story about a woman who had been raped. She was abused badly. It was clearly an act of violence. I am not entirely sure of the details here, but the result was that the victim of rape insisted that the experience of violence be written about descriptively and graphically. And that her name be used. She wanted the act itself to be present in the story. She wanted people to read what actually happened, not some embarrassed, shameful male journalist who did not want to write about the power and the violence of rape. The reporter was a woman. The story was published with descriptive details of the violence of rape.

They acted clearly with the intention of. . . .

Making it real.

Making it real for the purpose of what?

Not escaping it, not escaping the responsibility for it.

Does that mean that you are also addressing the pervasive fascination of the American mind with violent characters?

Yes. Well, of course. You know people are drawn to this, and I want it to be painful.

What then do you think about Billy the Kid in The Ancient Child?

Oh, what a transition! [Laughter]

Isn't Scott precisely concerned with that?

You live forever with that incredible violent contradiction of taking up the persona. Oh boy, what a good essay!

The implied readers with that story—at least three: you've got a Western reader, a Native American reader, and then you have something like the popular-culture reader of the violence of Billy the Kid—all implied romances of the reader, not the author.

But isn't Scott terribly close to repeating the celebration of violence that has been going on in the West?

No, I don't think so. No, you mitigate but do not perpetuate violence.

No, but can't you perpetuate the celebration of it?

What is history then?

Supposing history is what anesthetizes us, supposing history is the aesthetic indulgence of violence that renders us potential victims of real violence, because it's presented in a context that makes perfect sense, and it's never graphic, it's terribly abstract. "We understand how horrible it was when . . . ," right? Let's be graphic. Let's talk about the genitals, physically and descriptively, that were carved out of human beings by the United States Cavalry; of what the blood looked like, what the knife looked like, the dullness of it; what they said when they were cutting, what it looked like when a woman's genitals were removed. I mean, these terrible descriptive acts. . . .

Can one even describe that? Can one even imagine that?

No, not really. But I was reaching for an extreme to make the point that nothing could be as extremely invalidating as the historical aesthetic apologies for violence. We never get the act itself. We never get a story that relieves us of our post-traumatic stress from the denial of an open discussion of violence.[26]

And we all bear this, you know.

But your texts try to sort of tear the veil away.

Yes.

Again and again.

God loves you in literature.

---

26. *So—another opposition here: that between literature and history, with the latter associated with a type of lie, and the former with a type of truth, or with the task of trying, at least, to point towards it. The utopian function of literature in a residual form?*

History is ironic literature. The irony is the extreme absence of the "author" of historical narratives.

THREE

Jeannette Armstrong

Shall we start with that first question whether you find it problematic in any way that a non-Indian critic is doing these interviews? Would you feel differently towards an Indian critic? Would you feel more comfortable?

No, I don't. One of the reasons I feel that this process is important—that the interview process is important—rather than you writing and you interpreting, is that my view and my perspective is being respected. I think that in any crossover between cultures, whether we are talking about literature or any other kind of information, of knowledge, that process which solicits the other perspective is important, and I guess in as original a form as possible. Interview is one of those ways, and I think that the process itself is able to transfer that information, possibly in my mind without the kind of prejudice which takes place in a more formal kind of essay format or a more formal kind of written format. The interview to me is much more personal and more friendly, in person.

In this context, where does the notion of the group come in? We tend to look at Indian literature frequently, of course, as one in which there exists a special relationship between the text, the author, and a group. How do you view this aspect?

I think it's one of the problems that I have tried to put some clarity around in my own critical writing. I feel that this may be done much more in Canada and in the U.S. than it is from the outside, from other countries such as Switzerland or Germany.

One of the things that happens is that Indian literature, or Native American literatures, are lumped into one category as though there *were* such a thing, rather than many different cultures producing different kinds of literatures, and particularly different kinds of literatures as a result of contact with different kinds of peoples from Europe and from other parts of the world. And I think clarifying that and speaking about that creates a better sense of those literatures and their variety.

In relation to the group I know that there *are* commonalities, there *are* similarities that run through thematically. They run through our literatures because of our commonalities of experience in terms of the colonization process, both in Canada and the U.S., and the contact with European cultures and its effect internally on our people's traditions, and from the outside there has been an impact in the non-Native community, which is reflected back in a distorted way that we have to deal with. We call those "stereotypes," and those occur in many different forms about us as a general group, and so there is a part in our literatures which deals with that and has a commonality and a common theme and a common root.[1]

So that you would refer what one might call "pan-Indian" aspects to postcontact history rather than to similarities among the cultures before contact?

In literature I would. In literature I would, principally because of the influence that the English language has had in all of us, right across the board, except for the Quebecois—I mean, within the boundaries of Quebec, those First Nations people who are now speaking French and not speaking English.

Does that mean that there is a real barrier within the Canadian Native scene between English-speaking and French-speaking authors?

I understand that that barrier is not so much there between the Native peoples but very much between Native peoples and the French, and vice versa.[2]

1. *Commonalities would then in part be quite generally due to similarities in historical experience, and in part specifically and reactively to negative experiences such as exploitation and stereotypization?*
Yes.
2. *I have cut here, in the beginning of the paragraph, a phrase that seemed to indicate that at first you were going for English/French or anglophone/francophone differences within the Native scene. Any second thoughts?*
Yes—there are some barriers because of the French/English cultural difference in colonial history and Native experience as well as the barriers between the Anglo-speaking and French-speaking Natives, but the experience is largely a common experience of stereotypization and acculturation.

At this point I think one could ask the question in how far a shared colonial and postcolonial experience may also connect North American Indians with indigenous people in other parts of the world? Do you see concrete relations, concrete contacts that are being exploited?

That's very interesting, because two years ago we organized a conference. . . . En'owkin Centre was one of the three hosting bodies and organized an international indigenous conference of writers, performers, and visual artists. We came to that conference with the idea that there were commonalities between those indigenous people from countries that were colonized by the English, principally, that have relevance in terms of our literature. And indeed we found that to be so. We brought people from New Zealand (Maori writers and artists and performers), from Australia and those countries in Central and South America where there were influences by English tradition, and there were also two countries that we brought people from in South Africa and in the region of middle Africa.

And we found the commonalities there to be surprising: the same kinds of themes in the literature and then the same kinds of concerns in terms of perspective toward colonialism and in contemporary issues. There were the same battles, principally, that we were fighting to bring ourselves, as writers and as people who are carriers of their own literatures, forward through colonialism, fighting for that space to identify what those literatures are and how those literatures emerged, and not to try to emulate the literatures of the people who were colonizers, and to try to find the difference between the two and to try to state that difference to each other.[3]

I was trying to get to that now, and you have actually given me the lead: We've been alluding to Native literature in terms of the connections and similarities with others—connections and also similarities of course with English literature, with American literature, and with other Native literatures—and now comes this aspect of "difference from."

How much of a notion of cultural separatism, do you think, does one need to have in order to establish Native literature as something that is

---

3. *How specifically did you talk about literary strategies? And were there any similarities in that area?*

Not too specifically at the conference; however, a good networking exchange has resulted, which has resulted in exchange of literary strategy.

different from other literatures? This is also in reference to your own Native Creative Process.[4] *It seems to me that at least for certain purposes you do stress notions of separateness, of difference, very much.*

Sure.

That's something that I have been struggling with, with this writing school. The International School of Writing was founded principally from my understanding, and a collection of other writers from First Nations who are struggling with the same issue. One of the things that we could point to is that if—and I am talking about the school again[5]—if we take the writing school away and the students are put into literature classes or creative writing courses at universities that are mainstreamed for people who are coming from the background of the European literary canon, or the British literary canon, or the American (as different from the Canadian) literary canon, what we are principally doing is shaping the ways of that literature away from where it arises and from where the root of that literature has sprung, in terms of a written literature. And if we look at that [root], and look at the stages of change in terms of communicating through the literature that has occurred since contact, and then we wish to look at what was there before contact—we may not be able to say, "Boy, what was there before contact!" but the remnants that remain do emerge in the literature continuously, as well as social constructs[6] which promote a certain way of dialogue and a certain specific

4. *Douglas Cardinal and Jeannette Armstrong,* The Native Creative Process: A Collaborative Discourse, *with photographs by Greg Young-Ing (Penticton: Theytus Books, 1991).*

5. *You are anxious not to foreground yourself (or any other individual) too much. Is the school really envisaged as a communal effort? How far can it be that? What would that entail in terms of structure and procedure?*

Yes. It entails that the writers who come to teach influence the structure and procedure through consensus seeking and continuous dialogue related to the "Native perspective."

6. *Much more than the other authors, you tend to link literature and social practice. And it becomes quite clear that the connection is not primarily mimetic (literature does not primarily represent reality), but is something else. How would you describe the link? You do use the term "approach" a little later: what does it entail?*

Primarily, that the "voice" of social practice is shaped through dialogue, rather than literature being a reflection of social practice. Discourse is then a process rather than a product, and should be seen as the focus of study.

way of perceiving the interaction with not only people but the rest of creation, I guess. That becomes paramount in terms of a fundamental difference, and a fundamental difference therefore in the literature, in the way that literature itself is shaped and in the way that the approaches to life behind the concepts are shaped.

And so *that* becomes to me an essential and a fundamental reason to support the emergence of the literature and to support the creation of that difference, for, if you are looking at it in reverse, looking at the reasons that that difference occurs, it is because of the sociocultural context and of underlying philosophical ideas that permeate, and because of the different approach to life, and so you are getting right down to the essentials of what literature is about. And so to me that difference then is critical to preserve and critical to promote, and critical as well for *this* process of differentiation to take place.

Let me ask a semi-naive question. You're referring to the lived culture as the source of literature. What do you need a school for, then? Where does the formalized process of schooling come in, and isn't the establishment of this sort of school in itself already a decisive adaptation to Western notions of literature, Western notions of teaching literature?

I probably would like to use the term that Ivan Ilich uses: "de-schooling." That is a better word. Because what happens is that you are being schooled in English literature right from the time you speak it, you are being schooled in the British and the English and the American canon of literature right from the time you start reading the very first Dick-and-Jane reader. You are being schooled. And you lose consciousness in a sense, in English, of the parts that emerge from your own background of storytelling, your own background of different style and format, different rhythm and so on. Those become blurred in a sense or become indistinguishable from English as it's presented in various formats, whether you are talking of prose or poetry, or whether you are talking of nonfiction. So one of the things that I like to think about in setting up a school of this nature is that the structure that is there [in English] must be studied, but the de-schooling must take place in terms of looking at how that structure has permeated our own thinking and to show the students how our own literatures and our own styles and our own backgrounds can change that structure.

And so there needs to be a deconstruction process to liberate the voice of the writer as a First Nation writer, whatever First Nation they come from. And it is at that point that we start and we begin to look at the creative process in its real sense, in terms of where the students come from in their literature, whether they're rural, or whether they're urban, or whether they're Northern in terms of experience, or whether they are inner-city-made in terms of their experience. What are those experiences? What shaped those experiences? And where do the experiences go back to? Because we have that whole variety of Native participants in this program, and so that means you have that variety of voices arising all over North America.

The notion of voice, *I think, there brings together the idea of experience and the idea of expression.*

Where does the question of language and language change enter that particular picture? Where does it enter your school of writing and the process of schooling and de-schooling that you've been talking about?

I think that for me—I'm in the process of de-schooling myself about language. In other words, I've been studying the effect of the English language, not so much on me as a person and as a speaker of my language, but looking at the effect of the intrusion of another language on top of the language that is born out of the specifics of the culture, out of interaction with the land, interaction with the geography, interaction with each other in specific ways that are different from the interactions that give rise to English, for instance. And what I'm looking at really seriously is the impact of language itself on the psychology of how creativity occurs in that language.

Now, that seems like a really big project—I guess it is. That's what I'm engaged in at this point; I'm writing articles about it. But one of the things that I've come to sense is that language itself, in the way it is shaped from the past, creates a barrier and creates a really serious, maybe we could say "rigid," sense of what and how the world operates—that's the best way I can put it. And for the Native person, whether they speak both languages or are unilingual in their mother tongue, or speak English and have forgotten their mother tongue—regardless of either of those situations, the social context in many instances, on reservation or off the reservation—

how we interact, how we do things differently, how we feel in relation to how we do things differently—those things come up against the context and the subtext that are there in the English language, even in words and their meanings: the meanings of words that we cannot find in English any equivalent for, and the meanings that lie behind those words in terms of social context, interaction, thought, feelings, philosophies, and so on.

One of the things that I have some sense about—I guess I reached some sense about—is that it's not only going to be critical for our people to be able to almost re-hardwire themselves through literature to be able to understand *clearly* the effects, or *better* the effects, that colonialism has had on our people, because now the subtexts and the contexts in English (in terms of meanings and in terms of language)[7] don't contain some of the things that we do in our communities, in our societies. And those things need to be given words and need to be given contexts in terms of story, and need to be exchanged and shared through literature. Principally [in the past] it was storytelling, now it's through literature, so that we can learn from each other what our stories are, and how those commonalities run. And that's possible in English; it's not possible in our original languages.

Why not? Why is it not possible in the original languages?

Well, you have something like five hundred original languages that we would each have to learn. It's not going to be possible [eloquent sigh] for me to learn five hundred languages.

So you don't foresee a concrete future for literatures in the original languages. Is the basic statement then, if you want to have literature you've got to have it in English?

No, I didn't, I didn't, make that assumption. [Laughs]

OK, then let me rephrase it: How much of a literature can one have in the long run in the original languages? I mean, the question probably ties in with the additional question of the fate of programs to reinstate the original languages.

---

7. *The distinction recurs, between "meaning" and "language." Is it only that between "content" and "form," or is something else hidden behind it?*

I think the distinction is something more (beyond content and form) in that language *functions* differently in the cultural/social context, regardless of differences in content or form.

That's interesting because this last month we organized one of the first advisory forums of writers who are actually writing in original language, writing texts in the original languages.

Only in the original language? Or do they write simultaneously in the original and in English?

Both. They write both. But the forum was to bring together those writers who write in original language. All of them also write in English.

The idea of bringing the forum together was to ask what the questions are that those writers are faced with. And how can we provide an advisory to the government-supported programs to help understand and support the first-language writers, of First Nations in Canada? (We are talking about the Canada Council of the Arts and other kinds of support organizations like that.)[8] And one of the things that we saw immediately: there was the question of how the variety, just the sheer numbers of languages different from each other, interferes with that process. We are not talking about three or four principal languages at hand, we are talking, you know, two hundred and eighteen different languages in Canada alone, and where you can see people are writing in original language, you can see what they are struggling with in their own community, from that forum. They are struggling with the numbers of people who may be literate and who can read in that language. . . .

And who want to read. . . .

And who want to read in that language. And the other side of that question is, What have they had available in that language, and what will writing in that language from, say, grade one upward, from the Dick-and-Jane level upward, do to change the attitudes toward our own languages?

That was discussed, that was the priority of discussion, and one of the things that became clear was that English *is* permeating, English literature is permeating, our children's thinking at a very early age. There is no reason why our own languages cannot do

---

8. *Do you see any way that creative writing can be liberated from the often inhibiting influence of those funding agencies—without which very little could at present be achieved?*

More participation by writer groups like First Nation writers of first language in the development of the selection-jury process and criteria.

the same thing at a very early age, and that supports the writing not for the external cultural groups but for the internal . . . for the language group itself. And that in itself was one of the strongest reasons, because, Why should we worry about whoever else is going to read it? We should be worrying about who in our language groups shall be reading it and shall be benefiting from that. And in that, one of the things that became clear thus was that the colonization process, the assimilation process is achieved through language. That's the reality of it; it's achieved . . . disempowerment of our people was achieved, through language and is continuous in that process. And if we are going to change some of the conditions socially, in the social context in our communities, we have to change it through language, we have to change the education system, in a sense, in our own communities. And I'm not talking about the whole structure of public schooling or private schooling, I'm simply speaking about the language of communication as language of instruction.[9]

What about the economic side of publishing, etc? Does that interfere with the process significantly? Or do you find the more recently available media help you there, like desktop publishing and things like that?

Of course, the conclusion that we came to is that publishing is essential to that process, and so there is an important link that must be understood.

Theytus *has* been asked to convene a meeting of self-publishing, desktop-publishing, educational publishing groups across this country. There are many of them, people that are publishing readers and books for classrooms, and who really can see the potential in that in terms of how it can be used for wider distribution internally in their nations. And so that convening of that group of people will not just be a convening, it will be a working session in terms of how exactly, as a collective, we could regroup to support each other in self-publishing and desktop publishing and, where that capacity doesn't exist, how can this other group support that group and those other groups who don't have that capacity. But almost everyone has that capacity, except for very small groups, which can trade off or can work within a cooperative. And that's

9. *And do you see a first generation of competent teachers emerging?*
Yes.

one of the things we are actually looking at: setting up a cooperative style of publishing for that purpose. That doesn't have a lot of relevance in terms of public markets and the mainstream, but will require the financial and policy support of programs such as Canada Council of the Arts, and there are corollaries in each province.

We've been slipping into ever wider notions of literature actually, and what we are talking about here now is literature for the first grade plus a lot of other stuff. Do you see texts, from those that are being produced for first grade to your own poems, for example, as a continuum, as one big continuum of literary texts? Or would you distinguish among kinds of literature, like high/low, for use/for pleasure, or whatever?

That's interesting because the writers who came to that conference and were talking about literature, were talking about readers for school, although in my critical analysis that's not different. The stories have a different academic[10] language attached to it, but the stories in terms of their text and their texture are not different whether or not they are for a person six years old that's reading it. The reason for literature remains the same, which is *story*, basically.

And I guess one of the things that I saw there among the people who were writing poetry, the people who were writing short stories, was the excitement about the ability to use terms and to build concepts that are just not available in English. . . . One poet in particular read this poem in Micmac—and I don't read Micmac or understand Micmac, other than a few words because I have a couple of Micmac students here—and one of the things that he did was, he translated it into English, but translated it not as a word-for-word translation, but translated it poetically. It was astounding, the effect on everyone there. All of the people that were there weren't Micmac, but all of the people there that listened to the reading, listened to the interpretation afterwards— and he worked a while on the interpretation . . . he couldn't have achieved, we know that, he couldn't have achieved that particular

---

10. *What does the term "academic" imply here?*

The use of terminology which is learned and constructed through various levels of vocabulary acquisition.

poem if he had started from English. And I guess that's the best reason to us for saying that those literatures will grow, those literatures will be appreciated not just by that internal group but by others worldwide.

And I think it's really important to think about all that in terms of *that* communication outward to other groups of peoples, who appreciate literature for what it is, and other languages.

I think that's a very interesting approach—not just to talk about the language in which a text ultimately appears, but to talk in terms of the language from which it originates. What I think was perfectly obvious in what you said just now: there is a possibility then of translating into another language from which, however, the same kind of meaning could never have originated. I think that's probably a very good argument for the attempt to use more and more of the indigenous languages for the literary process itself.

In all senses literature opens up an inner eye in the reader or in the listener into another way of seeing the world, another way of understanding the context of the world. And from these Native languages, that's what happens: another way, another context of seeing the world, becomes possible.[11]

The process of translation will then of course always also contribute to an enrichment of the language into which the particular text is translated. . . .

How important is concrete factual knowledge about any Indian group to your own writing? How much knowledge do you expect your readers to have?

None. [Laughs]

I think if you're thinking clearly, you are writing from that. You're writing from that as a writer, you're writing from that perception. If I'm in the writing school assisting my students, I tell them I don't expect concrete knowledge. You're writing for a group of people who have a sense of, maybe, geographically where you are from and a sense, maybe, that there are some differences. But

11. *There two differences: that of literature (vis-à-vis everyday language and perception) and that among cultures, languages, and literatures. Is the implication that the difference that makes (for) the literary is realized differently in different languages?*
Yes.

145

they'll have a bigger bag and collection of stereotypes, which isn't knowledge or concrete fact, that your speaking in your voice is going to topple their stereotypes in terms of their belief systems about you, about your culture, and about your world view and about your thinking, and therefore about your literature.

So the implied reader of all those writers' texts would then primarily be the non-Native reader?

If the text is also for Native readers, then we are also talking about only that group with that culture that would have that knowledge. . . .

So that's where the multiplicity of Indian groups comes in once again. . . .

Yes. I have friends. . . . For instance, although I know geographically where the Seminoles reside, and I know in a very general sense maybe what their environmental conditions might be like, I have no sense of their interaction internally in their culture, and they would have to assume for me the same as for you, or they *should* assume for me the same as for you: that I don't know anything about them. In the context of their literatures they should simply assume *that*, other than for their own people. And I as an Okanagan would take that stance, that anyone, even our bordering neighbors, for all their proximity, are still not Okanagan, they still are not part of our cultural group. In English, that would be so. However, if I'm writing in Okanagan, then the reverse of that to me would be necessary. Then it's up to everybody else to try to find a way through. When a person from any other country of the world writes about, let's say, a rural situation, they are not writing with the intent of explaining themselves, they are writing with the intent of explaining that situation, and it's up to everyone else to try to find a cultural context to that end.

In good literature that cultural context should be provided.[12]

12. *Are you here first establishing a distinction along a line separating audiences and literatures and languages (as if one writes "for inside use" and "for outside use"), and then collapsing that distinction?*

No, I think not. How language provides cultural context is what literature in its best sense is; however, for the "outsider" there are fewer contextual givens (which need no reference in the text) than for the "insider," which changes the approach, texture and format, etc.

So you are viewing literature primarily in terms of communication, of going out, of opening up. There are texts at this point in time—I am concerned particularly with such texts from the South Pacific—that use terms from indigenous languages that you could not expect the non-Native reader to be familiar with, and they do not explain them, neither internally through references in the text, nor externally through glossaries. It is as if they went through a gesture of saying, "OK, if you want to know what this means, then go to the dictionaries; this text will not give you the information." How would you view this sort of text?

You are talking about English?

English, yes, with some Maori words in there that are not being explained.

One writer that I had here who was writing with a lot of technical terms in Micmac was struggling with that question. I struggle with that as well, and I asked the person, Lorne Simon; I said, "Who are you, and who is *your* intended audience for this text? Write with as much clarity for that intended audience as you require for it. If your intended audience is your own people, then write with as much clarity as is necessary for that purpose and, you know, live with the consequences of the rest of the world not understanding—as long as you understand that, and as long as you understand that at some point as a Native writer, as a Micmac writer, your text is going to be under observance by other people who are studying Native literatures and the question will come up."

I said, "I know that there are people outside of Canada and the U.S. who don't even know the Canadian terms that are widely used by Canadians in their English, and those people will be asking, 'What do these mean? What are they? What could this thing be?'" And I said, "If you are thinking about your book potentially being around for a hundred years or so as well, you may be wise to think about things that are not included in the English dictionary or the *Encyclopaedia Britannica*; you may think about providing a glossary of terms for that purpose. Unless you're thinking that this book is only going to be around for the next few years, you should think seriously about that."

And so that is one of the debates and questions we have had, and I think providing some kind of glossary, or providing some kind of a definition of terms in that sense, may be a wise thing to do, although in terms of the literature I don't think it is necessary.[13]

It's a hard question, I guess. If in some way it impedes the actual storytelling, the literature,[14] there's two things that should be considered: how better to do it so that it doesn't impede the creative process and the text in terms of literature itself. There should be clarity. I mean, that's the thing that should be foremost with every writer: clarity for every person, whether it's people who are from that cultural group or not. Clarity is to be striven for because you are writing for the reader. [But, secondly] if you are not writing for the reader, then you are not publishing, or you shouldn't be publishing, you should be keeping it in your diary for yourself.

There is, of course, the idea of writing for certain sectors of the audience in the sense of making them conscious of problems, maybe even insulting them; of not writing in terms of communication so much, or perhaps writing then in terms of communicating something like aggression. And couldn't this gesture of excluding the reader on one level, by one's choice of terms, help? Giving, as it does, the text a certain degree of "bite," of aggressiveness?

Well, I would put myself in the position of the reader. Let's say, for instance, I want to know something about South Africa, and I want to know something about how the indigenous people in South Africa think and feel in a contemporary sense, and I want to be able to understand that, and someone says, "Here is the text; it has a lot of indigenous words in there, but it might be helpful, you know," and I read it. I don't think I would go very far in the text if I were reading through a text that had a lot of indigenous terms and words which didn't have any meaning to me. I couldn't

13. *You are returning to a position of ambivalence about the question. Does this have anything to do with the fact that a certain hierarchy seems implied? Is to provide a glossary a gesture of propitiation?*

No, the use of terms which are unfamiliar should not be intrusive to meaning for the *intended* audience, and to a story/text true to that purpose, but it may be *useful* to provide a glossary if you *care* about *other* readers.

14. *"Literature" and "story": how far are the two synonymous? They often seem to be here. Any implications?*

I didn't say story, I said storytelling, which means the *process*, which, to me, may be synonymous.

continue reading it; I would therefore put it down as literature.[15] Now, if I were reading it, and the literature itself was speaking to me, and the words and terms that were being used were not impeding that, then I would read it all the way through. So I guess it depends on the expertise of the writer, and comes down to the ability of the writer to overcome the shortcomings of language, in a cultural context, through literature.

I think you have used a similar argument before, an argument that separated the level of expression from something deeper, something more real? "The literature itself"?

[Assenting noises were made all through that question.]

Could you explain this separation?

No, I have a difficult time too. I guess I'm spending my lifetime trying to explain that difference, but I'll tell you what I think so far about it and next week I may change my mind.

I think that there is that part of us as human beings that has a language that isn't contained in specific sounds made by different groups of people, but that has a language that we hear in music, we see in visual arts, or dance or performance, and that has a language that's particularly and specifically and uniquely human.

. . . And universal?

And universal. Although I'm not sure about that: I don't know anybody outside this universe [laughs], but I guess, universal in terms of the planet. It seems to me, this is what I think. . . .

. . . Not culturally conditioned by the particular cultural community?

No. I have this sense that there is a basic consciousness that has *a* language which overrides the different experiences we each come from, and that results in our literatures—or does not result in our literatures, but that we strive for in our literatures, in our

15. *Or as information? Is comprehensibility what makes for the literariness of literature? Don't the next two sentences establish a slightly different perspective?*

No. Not as *information* but as *informing,* as process through use of all that which makes literature an *experience* which gives meaning, rather than *comprehensibility.* If unfamiliar terms impede that for *me,* it is not because of lack of literariness, it is because I lacked the "ear." If the writer wants or needs *my* "ear," the writer creates the right sounds for my particular "ear" in as skillful a manner as is desired for the experiencing of it.

art, in our music, in our dance, in our performance. And when we somehow reach that moment in which that communication is made, we all know it. We all feel it when that connection is made, and it's finding maybe a pathway in that consciousness that the writers strive for, the performers strive for.

I know that sounds a lot like the European version of literature in terms of literary canons and so on, but I think seriously that, in terms of communicating across cultures, that's the language that communicates, that's the way that cultures are bridged, that's the way that difference becomes similarity, that it becomes common between people because people experience emotion in the same way—people experience rage no different from each other, they experience joy, they experience the kind of experiences we have when we have a religious experience that transcends all other experiences. The expression of that, and the reaching for that experience and being able to transmit that, that is, I think, where I'm drawing the difference. When that occurs, and when that is achieved, then we are speaking about another level of communication, rather than simply the communication of the everyday, the communication of the things that we do with each other.

Now, where with regard to this universal ground of experience, this universal sameness of experience, does your notion of the Native creative process come in?

It's one of the points of discussion that I had with Doug Cardinal, who is the person I was doing the discourse with. In speaking with you, and I suppose with anyone else from the European culture, that's where it becomes difficult for me to tell you what I really think, to tell you and explain to you what I really understand, because there is this curtain between us. And the curtain has a lot to do with belief systems and with the whole notion of a mechanistic society that's basically come to a pinnacle of belief that says nothing exists unless you can quantify it, and unless you can measure it, and unless it has some validity in the physical sphere of reality. And that's, I guess, principally where that question takes me in terms of the Native creative process, because as an Okanagan person—I won't even use the word "Native" because I can't say that other peoples that are First Nation, first people in North America, or other indigenous people, have this belief or understanding—I know that the world as I see it, and the world that I work from in terms of my writing, my literature, my art—principally where art comes from—has a basis that is not accepted or acceptable in terms of the belief systems of the European mind, the Western mind.

And that's where the difficulty lies of creating literature that occurs from that level and that is working, I guess, from that level in terms of our overall oneness of spirit, or oneness of mind, oneness of creation, or whatever. We, as Okanagan people, think about the arts in a very different way than the Western mind does. We especially think about sound, poetry, music, and dance in a very different way than the Western mind does. I can't say I know *really* how the Western mind thinks about it, but I know that for us it's a solicitation of the universal, it's a bringing inward to ourselves, a pulling inward of the universal, and then a reflection back outward again. So, to put it really simply, in my thinking the Western mind takes—I'll use visual arts as an example, and as a way of speaking about it—takes a material and attempts to spiritualize it, attempts to create it in a way which speaks about the spiritual—and that's the perception I have about it—whereas the Okanagan person will take the spiritual, the understanding, and the connection with the spiritual, and the attempt is to materialize that, to bring that forward into the physical plane, because it's not knowable, it doesn't have voice in the physical plane. And so when we materialize that, we bring it into a physical plane, either through words or through movement or through carving or through paint or through social construct.

That's what the discourse [with Douglas Cardinal] revolved around: that that activity is much different in process, so that the action of creating then becomes almost a religious experience, it becomes a spiritual experience, it becomes an experience of connecting to the spiritual and bringing forward from the voice that we say is within us, the voices of the grandmothers, the voices of the spirits, the voices of all the living things around us, the voices that speak to that part of us that's universal. And we make valid those voices in the physical world, where they resided in the spirit world. Without requesting conversion of anyone around, what we are saying is that we hear these voices continuously. They permeate, they make themselves known in the interaction between humans in moments of glory, and in moments of unique interaction, experience, and so on; they make themselves known. And if we as persons, like using a butterfly net, could capture that moment, and we could bring it forward, and if we can reproduce that moment, that spiritual connection that it has to all of other life, all other human beings, then that's the *process* which requires for us, for me as an Okanagan person, a different method than me taking some paints and saying, "What am I going to put on this canvas today?" [Laughs]

But in terms of what we talked about earlier the product of this creative process should and would be accessible to everyone.

[Assent]

. . . If it comes out all right. Is the implication, too, that the Native creative process in your view is the better approach to this underlying human universal level of experience than what you have described as Western creative processes?

I'm reluctant to make a judgment, because I'm not sure about the Western creative process. I know that the Western process ultimately at some point achieves that, has to achieve that, through its great artists, great writers, and so on; and so it's not a question of better or worse, it's a question to me of looking at the Western process—or not the process, but the reason (I guess that's what it comes down to) for creating things that ultimately become products like literature, music, art, and so on. A big and unhappy part of me says that a lot of the creating is done not for that purpose, but is done for materialistic purposes and that. . . .

. . . most of it of course is secular in spirit. . . .

[Assent]

. . . and that impedes those artists who need the liberty, and who require the liberty, to work with that universal voice. That doesn't stop them from working, but it impedes in many, many, many situations those great artists who might have been, who never were allowed, and who will never be; and instead it elevates others who are popular, pop artists, trinket makers, and so on, in a sense.

But I. . . . That's what I find problematic, from a pure creative sense: the liberation to not have to have any of that [other "art"] or deal with any of that—that to me should be socially possible in any society, but it isn't. Even today in our Native society it's not possible. People live in a wage and market economy, almost the world over. There isn't support for arts in a real sense. There is a materialistic kind of support for those artists who somehow make it in the market, and Canada Council, for instance, like anybody anywhere else, supports those artists who are successful in that sense. And that's where part of me says I'm unhappy about that situation. It's not saying it's better or worse, because I think the artist's voice will come through all of that muck, you know, and it does—but less often than it should, and perhaps not to the extent that it could.

You have alluded to modernization just now, in a way: seculari- zation, modernization, market economies, and all that. To get back to the more general cultural scene within which Native literature exists: if we accept that Native literature is also at least in part written for Native audiences. . .

[Assent]

how much change can this audience accept with regard to notions of Indianness, how much stability does one need as a background in order to feel that one has an on-going, continuously on-going, identity? It's this question of tradition and change, stability and change, that I'm interested in.

It's a really serious question. It's a good question in that, I think, many of the writers currently are grappling with this, and I see that much more in the last ten years with the writers that are emerging. I see that as a question that is being put on the table, so to speak, for everyone to examine and look at and speak about in their turn, whatever they may be writing about. And I think different writers have handled it differently. I think that probably in Canada the process is a little slower than it has been in the States because there *is* more literature, more prose fiction, in the U.S. that has been produced in the last twenty-five years than there has been in Canada. That's a reality, and, on the one hand, that creates a sense that there isn't any dialogue about it. But, on the other hand, one of the things in Canada that I noticed—let us say with Ruby Slipperjack in her last book, which I won't call a novel because I'm not certain that it is a novel—*Silent Words*—was that I felt that it required a Native consciousness about tradition and change to read. And primarily for the Native person reading it, whatever cultural background they came from, it required a certain knowledge about reservation life, and *rural* reservation life, and the subtexts running through it were concerned with the underlying questions of tradition and change and seeking of stability, and with finding your way within that, and a discourse around that.

That was evident in my reading. And I have not done any critical writing around that book, but I have talked to a number of non-Native critics about the book, and it went completely by them, it went totally by them in some cases. [Laughs] That's the one example. The other one is *Almanac of the Dead*, which Leslie Silko recently produced. I have been just doing a survey of my own and speaking to *knowledgeable* critics of Native American literatures, not only in Canada/U.S., but abroad as well, and I am finding the same reaction. The part that did come through was very negative, was a negative experience for them; but the larger subcontext totally went by a lot of the readers, and it required a Native contemporary person thinking in terms of world change and North American context and change, of globalization and the postmodern thought, in a sense, and deconstructive thinking, as far as all of the psychology that's presented there is concerned.

I found myself in some places thinking, How are they going to understand this? How are they going to read this, you know? And thinking, myself, This text is very deep and very difficult to get through, and in that sense it will be studied for years because of its approach and presentation, but primarily it will be studied by Native writers or Native critics, because of what it says and speaks. to in terms of *our* psychology, *our* lives.

And in terms of tradition and change, and how *I* think about literature and working with this writing school, for instance, I feel that the negotiation of change and tradition is one of the main reasons for going through with this, for me looking at each writer that comes here. I'm not too concerned about the devices or the crafting—although that is very important and essential in terms of fundamentals, crafting is, like anything else. If you can't craft well, nobody is going to pick it up and look at it. But what's more important is facilitating, not changing or not colonizing further, but facilitating the liberation of the voice and literature coming from *that* [Native] cultural context, *for two reasons*: one is, internally for our people, right across the board, *for the sake of our own reorganization in change* (in chaos, I guess) and of *identifying for ourselves the meanings*, socially and in terms of a subcontext, that run through the writings. *Identifying for ourselves our place, and therefore creating the kind of cultures* that we must become in order to survive as separate identifiable peoples with a heritage, with a culture and with traditions, and with a contemporary modern—if you want to use that word—approach. Approval doesn't have to be the same (or can't be) as the colonized mind; it doesn't have to be the puppet of the mainstream society in terms of the things that we are as a separate cultural group, whether we are talking about a larger group or a smaller group, in that which we entertain ourselves with, informing each other, and in our arts principally. So that whatever we make is not produced for mainstreamers, first is literature that's produced to inform and communicate that which is universal *among ourselves* and strengthening and stabilizing our . . . our . . . I guess you could say, our cultural context within a larger society.[16]

In many cases, of course, we are talking about groups in which at least many individuals have lost contact with a lot of their traditions, where a lot of traditional knowledge, quite simply, has been lost. How do you view attempts to reconstruct such knowledge? By going back, for example, to anthropological texts, to ethnographic texts?

Probably because of the way you are putting it, I differ with you. Maybe if you were to rephrase it, I might not differ with you. But I don't think a lot has been lost. I think the loss in material culture is perceived to be a loss of culture. We may be wearing blue jeans and T-shirts with slogans on them and eating hamburger, or whatever it may be; and as for material culture, we are living in housing like everyone else, and using electricity and watching television, and so on; but I think that if you go into a Native community, whether it's right in the middle of Vancouver or a Native community up in the North—and this is where I am saying the commonalities occur—you'll find that the culture, the

16. *We never got to the second one: External?*
Yes, the second is the external as a discourse outward to mainstream, to inform and neutralize the harmful stereotyping and myth making.

traditional culture of the people, permeates their lives in terms of what values they have and how they interact with each other, and the constructs that occur. All of that in a modern context, so that, whether you go to Toronto or you go to New York, wherever a group of Native people gather, you'll find them doing almost similar things, inducing the perception of pan-Indianism, because the similarity draws on customs of, say, the Plains people. We have powwows in the middle of New York or up in Alaska where, you know, obviously Plains Indians were not.

The thing that's underneath all of that material culture, the thing that is speaking there, is the culture itself in terms of communal gatherings and the kind of social support systems that occur within those communal gatherings, in the celebration of each other in those communal gatherings, or in sharing with each other. This is a cooperative communal lifestyle that isn't based in a market wage economy, in which people are required to be competitors, and [which] requires individualism rather than communalism. And you see that occurring everywhere: people gravitate—Native people, whatever culture they are from—gravitate to communalism; and whatever tool or mechanism they are using for that may be disclaimed as pan-Indianism, modern Indianism, or whatever, but underneath it all you'll see the same reasons for having it and the same values emerging, and you'll see the same story, the same subtext of a story emerging as to the reason why doing it is necessary for them in order to survive and be human. Whether it's in the middle of New York or Granville, they require that, they have to do that, they must do that in order to be human, in order to be. . . . It's not so much in order to be Native; it's that they, in terms of their internal values, require that kind of interaction, that kind of context, that kind of story, because the other story doesn't make sense. It can't make sense, because so much that is communal has survived. Its face has changed, and the material culture of it has changed, but the reasons, the underlying human reasons for it, have not changed.[17]

17. *The definition of "the culture itself" here has a lot to do with action—not with thought and belief in some splendid isolation, but with thought and belief as incitements to action, and as (primarily) expressed in action rather than words. Is this, too, why the notion of "story" is so important here—because stories are about people acting?*
Yes. The doing of it, the process, not the product.

I put it the way I did in part because I was once struck by the fact that a group like Native Earth, for example, in working on and in working out their plays that develop in the process of being staged—that they use masses of written material, they use masses of anthropological, ethnographic material, so that it seemed to me that their cultural activity did not develop primarily, or did not appear to develop primarily, out of the group context that you were describing, but it seemed to be very much via the written source, via the archive, via the library, in a way. So that then the reconstruction of group life that you encounter on the stage seems to be very much a reconstruction.

I agree with you, in *that* case.

You have referred to ethnic stereotype. How specifically does your writing encounter (counter, subvert—whatever) those stereotypes about Native people that are of course rampant in the dominant literature and the dominant language and the dominant discourses? And how do you, in your school, address that question?

I guess one of the most common things is our own stereotypes that we have built up ourselves about ourselves, that we draw on and use in all those things that sell well to the Western mind. [Laughs]

What sort of stereotypes specifically are you thinking of?

I'm thinking of a certain kind of construct that almost always emerges. I was thinking about Sherman Alexie's words, who was in the area lecturing—he said something like, every time a Native writer wants to be liked by the non-Native literary critics, they have to drag in a feather, and they have to drag in an eagle, or a buffalo, or somebody starts drumming and singing. They use those kinds of tools to provide a certain kind of stereotypical context, on the one hand, about tradition and Nativeness. On the other hand, there is the other [stereotype] about a certain kind of social context where social crises occur—the drunken Indian, for instance—and you see that stereotype used in many ways by *Native* writers.

In a sense there is a stereotyping of ourselves that emerges from someone else's stereotyping and reflects it. Because those are almost like passwords to get in, you use those stereotypes. Everybody can recognize them out there that's not part of the culture, and say, "Yes, I recognize that; that's an Indian"; and they become not only familiar, but they become almost taken for granted: that's the way it is. I mentioned Sherman Alexie because he is one of the most prominent on-coming new writers in the U.S. now; he is pointing out some of those stereotypes, and he is being really courageous in doing so, because in pointing them out to our own people, we say to them, those stereotypes are just as stereotypical, they are no different than *their* stereotypes.

And so one of the things that we have tried to talk about in terms of our discussion groups, our workshop, is to look at our own writing and to look at the kinds of stereotypes that we are drawing on, which occur in our writing simply because that's the easier way to present it. And I think that, as for myself, I was looking at my own writing critically trying to decide if—in the novel *Slash*, for instance, looking at all the characters, the secondary characters and of course the primary characters—whether or not I was presenting and perpetuating stereotypes, whether or not I was in a fundamental way drawing on and making those stereotypes become more real in the minds of our people and other people.

That's the question that I had internally, turning to criticizing my own work, and I guess in some sense with one character I thought that maybe I was indulging in that—not the primary character, but another character.[18] And I felt, going back and looking at it, if I were to do a critique, I would say that character represents one that's very familiar to many people, and that character was one that I could easily use *because* it was so familiar to everyone. And I find that it presented a stereotype, that I could have done better with that character, or done better by that problem that exists behind the stereotyping of that character. I could have revealed that problem and probably would *now*, rather than ten years ago, when this book was written. I think that occurs because, as a writer, it's easy to draw on and use stereotype. So I encounter that as a problem; I do encounter this as an obstacle, and I do recognize that sometimes we have blinders on as Native people because those stereotypes are so familiar. It's like picking them up and just using them, the same way as if you'd pick up a wrench and use it.

18. *Would you care to identify that character?*
No.

What's the alternative?

I think in the last few years one of the alternatives has been to question every character, every way that we pursue our writing. And if we know that this character is not real in terms of how things really are in our community and how things really occur in our community—in other words, the character is only real in that that's how other people have perceived it, but it was never a reality—*that's* what a stereotype is. Thus there isn't a basis for that character, it's a misrepresentation of something; and what is that "something"?

So true representation would then be. . . .

"True" representation is representation as best as possible. (Absolutely true representation is not possible because it is always only representation.) Then we can circumvent our own stereotype and, in a sense, not indulge in stereotyping. And I think that will produce better literature, and surprising literature, too. (To the Western mind this is the main thing in society.)[19] And I think in a sense that Leslie Silko has done that; certainly, the stereotypes are not there.

The question that some people would ask, then, is whether in the present state of Western civilization and of the English language true representation is possible at all in that language. The implication of what you have been saying is that, yes, given the proper approach, given the proper tools, true representation is possible.

It never is, but close to it.

OK.

[Pause]

This is a question that has always interested me: How does one react as a writer—or as an academic, of course—to the question of art and exploitation, academic life and exploitation? How does one react specifically to the charge that one exploits in one's writing—or in one's teaching—the cultural heritage of groups that are after all, many of them, severely disadvantaged.

That's probably one of the more serious questions running through our dialogue together as writers and artists and performers, whenever we have a convening among ourselves.

19. *What did you mean to say here?*
I was referring back to how the Western mind approaches literature within the context of society, in that literature is reflective of social process.

The question really is whether your school, for example, does not create a privileged elite.

It's a very difficult one because we are enmeshed almost without extrication in this Western market economy. It's difficult to liberate yourself from that and survive in terms of being able to actively participate and work in the art. You have to be able to sell your work, whether you are a writer or whether you are a visual artist; you have to be able to survive in the everyday mundane sense of making money at it, feeding your family.[20] That means in some sense creating literati, creating that group of people who are going to be the consumers of what you produce, and creating that consciousness where people desire to purchase what you produce.[21] And, in a sense, criticism, critical work, is done with that in mind: we want more people to read these books and teach these books and buy these books. And so a number of Native people who are producing need critics, need Native critics and non-Native critics, to do that.

And so a writing school like this definitely in that sense is engaged in "creating literati": a number of people who can communicate and provide critical analysis around creative thinking and creative work, how it emerges and how the differences occur. To interpret that to the mainstream public is necessary, and we have been engaging in that. And I think that in that sense there is nothing evil about it inherently, there is nothing wrong with that inherently. But when *that* becomes the sole purpose, and when that becomes the sole activity—marketing, consumering of the product, consumering in terms of what we are producing—when that's the sole purpose and that's the only reason why critical work is done, then we lose the whole reason we started the school to begin with. And the exploitation in that sense is a necessity for any art, for the

20. *The implication here would seem to be that the role of the "artist" has changed—and we have been close to this topic before. Do you have any further comments?*
No.

21. *A very sudden swerve from producers to consumers of literature: Why? What is the relation between the two in this context?*
I was commenting on the relation of creative writing to consumerism as art-exploitation motive. That is, to shape for product, rather than the process of literature shaping the social context.

reinterpretation and the saleability, I g
that's the way the world operates, now.

It didn't operate in that particu
societies, but it does now; and that's tl
grapple with that reality all the time ii
vidual integrity in the work that we prod
it comes down to purpose in terms of the
in the classroom, one of the things we p
vidual to look at their own primary pur
creative process, and to find within themse
their reasons are for producing. There are m
why artists produce. Some of the writers are
rage, anger, and a need to clarify; some of the w
ducing simply out of love for creating words and crea
and language, and creating stories, simply for the cra
there are many different reasons for them, and we are tapping
that purpose, into that reason, and strengthening that.[22]

*You are arguing primarily in terms of subjective integrity. Is there
also the aspect of what you might call "objective economic integrity"—
that the artist, once he or she becomes successful, maybe has to funnel
part of the material rewards back into the community—that sort of
thing?*

As I mentioned before, that is an interesting question. . . .

*I'm also asking that because the School of Writing, of course, is very
close to the Centre here and to Theytus, which is a community thing once
again.*

One of the interesting things we have found—and this goes
back to an earlier part of our conversation—is that the values of
the Native community, whether they are inner-city or whether
they are rural, are retained through interaction, in some cases in
really specific ways. What we found is that Native writers primarily find their purpose in sharing voice, and primarily find
their purpose in stabilizing and giving back to their community.
So you'll find writers not just engaged individually in writing, but

22. *And what are your own reasons? How, specifically, do you negotiate the tension
you are here building up, between rage and love?*

Both, as I think in process they do not differ; however, in social context and
voice they do.

large segment of their community through their
whether it's in a concrete sense, as in this writing
Theytus here, or whether it's in a much less concrete
rms of political voice or rhetoric—that's one of the
t you'll feel: that in the Native context, what you are
ith, and what you have been given in terms of skills,
only belong to you. It belongs to the community, and it is
for the benefit of the community, to benefit the community
me way. And the responsibility of the artist is to ensure that,
ever much the artist is elevated, the community alongside
ust be elevated as well and must benefit as well.

And I don't think that that has changed; I don't think that that
has become different. I look across the border and I see all the
Native writers engaged in that, engaged in one way or another—
and perhaps beyond that many other conscious, thinking people
from other than Native communities have that same consciousness. I'm not saying everyone, but I'm saying we see that as one of
the underlying features of being an artist in some way. And that
has something to do with the joy of creating and that spiritual
place, as we call it, that universal voice and universal connection
to oneness as we call it, sharing that with the community. There is
a feeling of such responsibility, and that feeling permeates the art.
And somehow in the Native community that seems to be a priority rather than on the back burner.

*I think that has gotten us into the area of the question of the
authority of the art. The implied implication then would be that part of
the authority of the art is drawn from this particular relation with the
community.*

*Let me interject at that point a question that I think comes much
later in the sequence here: What made you an artist?*

[Laughs] When you are mentioning the authority of the artist,
I've never actually even thought about it in that context. But that's
what it comes down to, that's what happens, when you present
and represent a social context in your art, so that many different
people from many different experiences come together in a commonality of experience and expression.

And I never thought about it in terms of authority, but that's
basically what it comes down to. And my thinking about what

made me an artist—I'm not sure. I know about my background as a child, and essentially I think I know how I was shaped to be an artist. Whether or not that [being an artist] is part of my own personality, something that a person is born and gifted with, I don't know, I have no idea. But I do know that as a young person, as a child, one of the largest influences on my life, as relates to my writing, one of the things that influenced me greatly was the access to storytellers, to the people who were the teachers in my community and philosophers in my community. Through their storytelling, they have provided their philosophy and provided the teaching and provided the way that my mind works in *my* language, in the Okanagan language. And it has influenced my thought process, to a degree which I know makes me an artist.

Were you privileged in your access to those people, to those teachers? Or was it just that you were more obviously affected by them?

Well, I was privileged, I was. The family that I belong to is a traditional kind of family, and they were trained storytellers all of them, and that going back generations. And besides this, besides the trained storytellers on my mother's side, the family also had responsibility of leadership—"leadership" meaning certain kinds of social awareness and social interaction. And in my father's family there was the responsibility of—I guess "medicine society" is the best way to put it in English terminoloy: people were keepers of ceremonies, and in that context it's not seen as leadership, but if you think about the church being a great influence on society in the Western mind, in our community the keepers of the ceremonies had great authority, though not in a dictatorial sense. . . .

Sure. . . .

. . . But had great influence and also had much knowledge about social interaction, about people and about different things that influence the people and about how things occur.[23]

---

23. *There is the notion here of "providing a context of meaning," "sense-making for the community," contextualization in the most general social sense, that is close to the functions we ascribe to artists. Where are the differences?*

Contextualization, yes, but beyond that a "creation," a materialization of something "new" which was somehow not discernible within the social context, or not present.

So, I was privileged in that sense in my family. I'm not the only one; I am talking about my brothers and sisters as well in that. We had teachers who came to our family and who were accessible to us, and who also were our mentors as we were growing up in terms of what the Okanagan mind is, what the philosophy is, what the stories are, what the knowledge is; and a big part of that is transferred through art, rather than, you know, through *lecture.*[24] [Laughs]

What I say is that a big part of that [knowledge] is transferred through ceremony, a big part of that is transferred through customs, through traditional customs that are art in the real sense. And I found myself, in growing up as a young person, thinking in a creative way. I saw myself as a maker of words and a maker of art early, very early, and a maker of statements—I guess, that's the way to put it—and thinking about the social context and putting it forward, this is how I see it. Because of all those factors: the leadership factor, the ceremonial factor, and the storytelling aspect.

So I was privileged in all three areas to be able to come up in a family which gave me that kind of skill and that kind of background. I think in a very real sense, in a very physical[25] sense, the training that I had very early on has really a lot to do with it, and every one of my brothers and sisters was exposed to the same thing. Each one of them has become a professional in terms of our community, the Okanagan community, in a different area, as well. They are recognized as much as I am among our people in those different areas. They are not as recognized externally, because their art doesn't extend outward as mine does. In a sense I can see in each one of them where the crossovers—the sameness of our teachers, the sameness of our mentors—created us as the people that we *are* in relationship to what we do in our everyday life.

For me, it's not just the writing that I do. The writing is about one quarter of what I actually do in my community and in other contexts. The creative process doesn't just include the writing; the

24. *Implications? Can one operate in terms of implication vs. explication, implied vs. explicit authority, and the like?*
Yes. Very much so, in that story or art in our perspective is a way sign *toward* something which the reader/viewer constructs.
25. *In terms of how to make physical the unseen and abstract.*

creative process includes putting this thing together in the En'ow-kin Centre, and putting together many other things that I have con-tributed to in terms of bringing back health into our community through the actions that I do, bringing benefit to the Native com-munity, and the non-Native community, in an act of looking at the creative process not just as a process of putting words on paper, but making and changing and transforming the physical reality around us.[26]

You have been talking about your several activities as really mutually reinforcing one another in being part of one single project. Do you ever experience any conflict between those different areas in terms of, for example, time limitations, limitations of energy, etc.—that you would wish to spend more on just one area.

I am a visual artist, primarily, that was my . . . I guess you could say, first love. From when I was a teenager, all the way through my college years and university, visual arts was some-thing I was obsessed with and spent a lot of time at. I found that I had to make some decisions after I left university about that, and the decisions have always been not unhappy decisions, but I have always felt short-changed, I guess, in the sense that those deci-sions had to be made at all.

Perhaps I could have pursued visual arts, but it requires full time. And the time that I *was* involved in producing visual arts, painting and sculpture, it took twenty-three hours of a day every day to work at continuously, and even then it was not enough, and I couldn't have spared time for other things that I wanted to do, needed to do as well.

And writing in a way is more compatible with the other activities?

It's more compatible because it's more transportable. It comes down to that: *physically* it's more compatible. I can pack a note-book with me, and I can create and write on a plane or on a bus or in my hotel room and wherever, while I'm doing all those other things. I can't, I couldn't, find a way to do that with the kind of

26. *This—since you are talking about the principle of "putting things together," of establishing contexts, of, in a sense, "making whole"—is quite general. Do you wish to add a few examples?*
An example I gave is En'owkin itself as a physical reality, an institution, a place instead of a story, a concept, an idea, or a potential.

visual arts that I was producing. And if I could have found a way I would have, I guess.

That throws an interesting sidelight on your poetry, this concern with the visual arts.

[Assent]

Some of my students have been worried by the representation of women—notably, but not only, white women—in some Indian texts at least. They've called that representation chauvinist. Do you have any reaction?

It's one of those areas—when we go back to the discussion of stereotyping—it's one of those areas in which one sees our own habit of stereotyping, our own internalized acceptance of that stereotyping that is in Western society about women. And when we look at the reality, the actual reality in our communities, in the Native communities, our own stereotyping is not even seen there. I know that, as a Native woman, as an Okanagan woman. Some of that chauvinism is prevailing much more—but I know that in the way it is presented and represented in the books, in the novels, that I read, only in very few cases has one moved away from the stereotyping.

And I think that as writers we *are* becoming much more aware of that, and much more seeking clarity around us. There are a number of women attending the school here creating dialogues around that among each other, and doing some critical work on it. When that critical work starts emerging, then change can happen, and I think maybe looking at the works of our people offers a few critical comments about that. And for me, it does occur to me to be negative[27] because I know that—going to Tomson Highway for instance—the stereotyping he uses is a prominent craft device, and so chauvinism is prominent, even if its use emerges as the other extreme of chauvinism. His crafting is so well done, and his knowledge of the format, the stage play, is so good that the subtext which emerges as a result almost can be accepted. My criticism addresses the question of the treatment of the female figure, but that is not restricted to Tomson: there are a number of other texts that I could pick up and say the same things about.

OK. This comment came out in a seminar of mine, for example in discussions of Scott Momaday's House Made of Dawn*:*

27. *Negative in which sense?*
That stereotyping is chauvinism.

Is the representation of non-Native, of white, people ever a point of discussion in your courses?

There has been recently a discussion around that. We had a really good discussion in one of the workshops at the recent Western Regional Circle of Native Writers around how the representation of non-Native people should be thought about, handled, and so on. I have had great difficulty, and the difficulty that I've had is not *wanting* the stereotype but, nevertheless, maybe stereotyping anyway because I can't seem to find any other way to look at non-Native people. . . .

The question to my mind in part is in how far certain situations that you want to write about do not automatically bring along stereotypical figures, who in real life would be stereotypes. Bring them along. . . .

That's the basis of discussion that we had. That whole question about [how], well, they *are* stereotypes. There *are* people who are haters of Indians, and all their actions are almost classifiable into a category. This is how they act, this is what they do, and this is what they look like; they are all beer-drinking, burping, red-necked people, and we all know them, you know. [Laughs] If that's a stereotype, then *is* it a stereotype if there's six hundred of them around, surrounding every Indian community? And everybody knows them, you know. That's the questions that we discussed. They probably. . . . I don't know, maybe *stereotype* is not the word for it then. Maybe "archetype.". . . [Laughs]

Yes, if you think about stereotypes in terms of something that's opposed to reality, then certainly stereotype is no longer the word. The opposition stereotype vs. reality breaks down.

[Assent]

So I guess that's one of the areas that I have had some dialogues and discussions on. I have not used non-Native characters to a great extent in any part of my writing. I consciously stayed away from it; I attempted not to. . . .[28] I think in everything that I have written maybe one non-Native character emerged. In *Slash* I presented a

28. *This would create a sort of "representational separatism" that looks very odd alongside the discursive interculturality of many Native texts—and your own ones. Are there areas of representation that seem to become discursively "impossible" in certain cultural (social, political) situations?*
Yes, I believe so, but it is not clear enough to me to discuss here.

very, very minor, third-level character. Even that character is in my mind a *real* stereotype, the environmentalist who works with the Native people. They are always there and everybody knows them, people are familiar with them, and their reactions are pretty much the same.

But what could I have done that's different. . . .

It brings us back to the question of earlier on, in how far one can avoid stereotypes. There are certain types of material that carry stereotypes along, not just verbal stereotypes, but stereotypical reality elements. . . .

[Assent]

Which of course then opens up that entire question of true representation once again. In order to represent that sort of reality you almost need then to employ a stereotype.

What I have not seen, and this is an area where this dialogue takes us, what I have not seen in Native literature is a Native person writing from [the point of view of] a main character who is non-Native, and in a serious way representing what that main character does and thinks and how that main character changes.[29] I have not seen that, and I asked my students, why is that?

. . . Why, in view of Big Bear and characters like that, right, being created by non-Native writers?

So we do some exercises around that. I asked them to write from that point of view, and it's hilarious sometimes. I think some of it should be printed because it's satirical[30] and usually ends up as a very, very poignant political comment in terms of how Native people perceive non-Native people, their actions, their values, and their thinking. It could be very revealing. It can also be construed as racist as well—which is what happens when a non-Native person does that.

29. *This is a thought that questions the entire interdiction on "appropriation of voice": can that specter be banned by working toward a mutual and equal crossing of boundaries, with Native writers "entering" fictional "white" minds, and white authors "entering" fictional "Native" ones?*

Perhaps, but in a racist world it can only serve to reinforce, it seems, instead of dispelling racism.

30. *Precisely! It gives one a whole range of writerly perspectives, between empathy and aggression, that otherwise tends to be closed.*

So I don't think you'll see that coming about, because the discussion around it is. . . .[31] Some of the students that I have had discussions with, and other writers, said they wouldn't do that. Maybe with a secondary character or a minor character they'd do that, but only to construct the reality of the main character and the main reason for the story. So that's as far as the dialogue goes. I couldn't say that I would consciously set about writing from that perspective unless it was for pure satire, which would be interesting, I think.[32]

It would certainly be interesting. And the implication of that appears extremely interesting, that there is an extreme barrier, at least at this point in time, between the two cultural groups, at the same time that both of them are using the same language. And that there is more and more intense awareness, among the groups, of the problems that are involved in interaction. And it's almost as if there was a barrier that is more impermeable from one side than from the other side.

[Assent]

It's an interesting exercise in discourse.

[Pause]

Do you find that Indian writing is characterized by writerly strategies that clearly make it different from non-Indian writing? If so, what are they? Would you recognize a Native text blindfold, so to speak?

I think I would, although there are a couple of examples in which I would say, no, I couldn't. Martin Cruz Smith comes to mind. I'm not sure that I would read that and recognize that as a Native text if someone had not told me—*Gorky Park* and other books. But when I was starting out the idea of the writing school, I thought about that question in terms of *what makes this text Native?* What is recognizable about it? We had Joy Harjo and Margo Kane and Lee Maracle and Mini Freeman and Tom King and other people; we got together here in En'owkin Centre and discussed that. Because *Nativeness* is fundamentally what we are talking about in terms of writing strategies.

31. *The discussion is too fraught with political dangers?*
Yes. This is the not very well articulated result, the *political oppression*, which it effectively reinforces and affirms.
32. *Clearly, you are tempted by the possibility. Will we be able to read some satirical work by Jeannette Armstrong soon?*
[No answer]

And we were looking at course work in terms of the programs itself, the programs that we would provide. We have to teach something to the students. We talked about writing and a strategy, the kind of techniques and approaches that they might take, and the thinking around those. So we did four days of discussion on that question. And I guess one of the things for me that comes through very clearly, regardless of the expertise in English grammar, is that in the structure of the language that's used, grammatically, one of the things it says immediately is, "This is Native." One of the things that for me is an indicator, is the structure of the language: in terms of dialogue and even in terms of nondialogue, how the writer is developing the use of language, the structure of the language—that tells me that this is Native. It probably has more to do with rhythms than anything that I could point to grammatically. And also the way that concepts and ideas are pursued in a philosophical context. That's the best way that I could put it.

[Tape changed]

We were talking about differences that you recognize in Native texts. We were talking about the philosophical aspect of the whole thing.

I guess the *essence* of what is being written about makes it recognizable as a Native text. I can't put a formula to that, but I do know that if I pick up an anthology, pick up a collection, or I look at a number of Native books on the shelves, that there are some things that I'm *not* going to find written about in there, and that *there* are books on a number of areas which are important to Native concerns. I would say maybe you could call those themes or perspectives that Native writers concern themselves with in their writing, which make it obvious that this is Native writing. I won't say there is a sameness about it, because it's not sameness that I'm talking about.[33]

I was interested in your comment about rhythm. Would you refer that sense of a different rhythm at all to the influence of oral traditions?

I think it could be that. I haven't come to that conclusion definitively.[34] I think it could partly be that, but it may not be in

33. *Any specifications? Any additions?*
No.
34. *Are you refusing to accept here what has after all come to be used as a critical stereotype—however much truth there may be behind it?*
I believe so.

some of the writers whose language doesn't exist any more, or who are not speaking that language, and/or who have been removed from that language for a number of generations. I'm not sure that original language and story, the oral tradition, has a presence in the kind of English that's spoken by Native people to the extent in which it influences almost every writer. I'm not sure of that.

There is, however, good indication that this is true: good indication that the transition English, sometimes called Red English, that's spoken on reservations is an oral form of English, spoken with a Native rhythm and a Native structure, enunciation, and so on. That seems to be a reality—that if you studied Reservation English you'd be studying a different form of English than Standard English or modern "straight" English, and that you would find, in the study of that, that there are certain kinds of sounds, rhythms, that permeate, and that have their roots in, the original language of those people and the oral speech patterns of those people. And I think that carries through, generation to generation, whether you are speaking English or whether you have a knowledge of original language or not—that carries through, that *pattern* carries through. So it does seem to influence to that extent.

What I am concerned with, though, is leaving it at that. I am not sure that it is that *completely*. There are some indications, from my thinking and my concern with it, that it also has to do with a philosophical approach to life and a *pacing* of that—I am getting into really difficult ground here, in finding the right words—but the different lifestyle that underlies the different philosophical approach creates, internally, a different rhythm and a different pattern, maybe in terms of where and how thoughts occur and become words, and how those words then become English words on paper, and how we make those choices to construct paragraphs and chapters and so on in books or poetry. That to me contributes a lot as well to the sense of rhythm, the sense of different rhythm, that's maybe present—as well as the contribution from the orality.

I made that comment regarding the oral tradition in part because I remember you once talking about Harry Robinson. Of course quite a bit of his material has become available, and I have been fascinated by these texts, by the way in which they operate totally differently from your standard written text: they constantly throw the reader back on his or her own resources trying to establish in one's own mind an oral situation, and then *one can follow it.*

He was an oral storyteller, and he was a master storyteller in our language. The text you are reading was spoken by him in English—he had a very limited knowledge of Standard English, and he used it very rarely. I in my whole life hardly ever heard him speak English, but I know that he as a storyteller was masterful in using what English he had to transfer that information that he did transfer to Wendy in the English that he knew.

In other words, he would normally not have presented the stories in this way?

No, he would not have spoken these stories in English. And I laughed. . . .

Which is significant in view of the fact that these stories have now become extremely important in the canon.

And it's funny because . . . I haven't done any critical work around this. I have been asked to, because Harry Robinson is one of my main teachers. . . .

That's what I remembered.

The stories that he tells in these two collections that were published by this anthropologist[35] are stories that are not Okanagan *stories* actually. They are stories that are contemporary. . . . They would be the things that people would tell informally, you know. In a sense they are the folk stories, the folklore, that exist about historical events and people and things that occurred. A few of the stories that have relevance within our real mythology and our sacred literature do sometimes get referred to by him in those stories. But reading those stories was kind of strange or funny because he stayed away totally from the real stories, the main stories, the sacred-literature stories that are told in our language.[36] When he told them, he must have spent hours and hours and

35. *Harry Robinson and Wendy Wickwire*, Write It on Your Heart: The Epic World of an Okanagan Storyteller *(Vancouver: Talon Books, 1989); Harry Robinson,* Nature Power: In the Spirit of an Okanagan Storyteller, *compiled and edited by Wendy Wickwire (Vancouver: Douglas and McIntyre; Seattle: University of Washington Press, 1992).*

36. *Would you care to comment on the distinction between types of stories that you are implying here?*

Not beyond what I have said here.

hours talking to Wendy, giving her these stories that are very important in their own right about our contact with Europeans and so on, in some of the humorous occurrences, you know, and anecdotal pieces that he provided.[37]

Because they are not traditional stories, I think, they maybe, paradoxically, become much more significant, much more useful to young writers as a link with the past.

In that sense I laugh—knowing Harry and knowing how he was—because he was doing the best that he could in English in the stories that he felt could be shared, or should be shared, and his choice making in terms of what the rest of the world should know was, from my point of view, really clear: because he was speaking to a non-Native person, he was telling these stories to a non-Native person. And my respect for him is tremendous in result of that, but it makes me laugh. . . .

Do you use those stories at all in your classes?

No, not usually.[38]

I have that question here about traditional Western genres. It seems to me that particularly Native North American literature uses traditional Western genres less frequently than other Native literatures.

Do you have any comment? I guess in a way this is also the question how important notions of genre are, once again in your own process of writing, in your own process of teaching.

[Sighs] I guess for me as a writer I hadn't really paid a lot of attention to that question. I consciously at some point said, OK, this looks more—*Slash*, for instance—this looks more like a novel,

---

37. *I am struck by a certain ambivalence here, as if you were, on the one hand, trying to reduce the importance of the material in English and, on the other, acknowledging it. There appears to lie a problem behind the whole thing. Would you care to comment on it?*

My respect for Harry and his choice to do this overrides my feelings about the "anthropological" purpose of how it is presented. There is a respect for his mastery of story and how it emerges, despite a feeling of his format being contrived by the recorder of his story, in a way which, for me, does not serve Harry's mastery.

38. *Why not? And you did not pick up my suggestion that they might be relevant as a connection with the historical past. Is there anything about them that you find disturbing?*

I don't use them because they fall short of what I know to be representative of how we use language, though they do reflect an anecdotal accounting of some aspects of a more recent history. Nothing disturbing.

and maybe could be edited and packaged that way. But even then the work I'm involved in now—I have been writing for the past year on a new work—I'm finding it very difficult to say where best it would fit, and I find that same sense looking at Lee Maracle's *I Am Woman*. Where does that fit? What is it? If you look through the text, there are many different things in there that are not anywhere near any recognizable genre; and so that difficulty arises, because there is such, you know, clear delineation between fiction, novel, and poetry, and so on. . . .

Where are these clear delineations?

In the Western canon, but one of the things. . . . I think that those delineations are constructs, more contemporary constructs, because if you go further back, they are not there. The novel is a relatively new thing, and certain kinds of poetry in terms of the way they are presented in a modern context are relatively new. Playwrighting is a little bit older, but even then, contemporary plays are different to a very, very great extent from plays three or four hundred years ago.[39]

So, in terms of what we are doing here at the school, it really depends a lot on your own understanding of your format. If you are thinking about a genre as a format that you can hang your thoughts on, be clear on what that is and why you are using that. It must serve the purpose of your voice, rather than you serving the purpose of that genre. In other words, you are not constructing a novel so that the novel is what the primary purpose is. If it works for you, if it's that format that is going to give your intent the integrity that it needs and give rise to the things you need said, then that's the format you use. But otherwise construct a format, and understand the necessity[40] from what that may be, and use that and argue for that. One of the things that I do know, for instance, in the Native oral tradition is that we have a difficulty because there is the pocket called "children's literature" and because of the percep-

---

39. *Could one then also say that you are concerned, at least in part, with over-coming an overschematic "division of labor" among types of writing by going back to an earlier, more open state—or by going forward to what resembles that earlier state?*

Just to a more open state.

40. *The necessity of what?*

The necessity of that particular format for the intent.

tion that some of our sacred literatures fall into that category, and the perception that there is a difference between children's literature and stories about. . . .

"Real" literature?

Yes [laughs], "real literature," stories that are for adults. And I say, for us there *was* no difference, there *isn't* any difference, and it takes really masterful storytelling to write to both audiences at the same time, or to tell to both audiences, without losing either or without catering to either. How do you do that? How did our storytellers achieve that? What are the tricks and techniques and devices that that storyteller used to do that? Find them, research them! Find out what those tools are and apply them in a story. Work up a story with which you can entertain someone who is fifty years old along with someone who is five years old, and create the deep, deep literary sense that occurs there, in those stories, when you do interpret them into our language. How is it? How has it worked? What is the crafting? And more importantly, how does this genre itself, how does it work? What are its parameters? What makes it work that way?

. . . So that you are there returning to a Native genre rather than to a Western genre, and the violation of Western limitations would precisely occur in returning to the Native genre.[41]

[Assent]

And that can be a very exciting literary work. The most exciting thing that I see happening in this school here is that students are pushing the limits of that and consciously thinking about genres as not being confined to the Western idea.

Have you found any Western genres specifically useful in your own writing?

Poetry, yes.

Well, the modern blank verse I find is useful, and I think that probably, for me, it provides the kind of freedom that I need. Free verse, to some extent, is wider open than blank verse, but I think blank verse has some of the kind of rigidity, maybe, that I need, that occurs in the traditional Native poetry from the Okanagan.

41. *Returning to a Native genre that would at the same time be defined as more open, more versatile than the Western one—right?*
Apparently so.

And I also find that, in the storytelling of our tradition, probably the literature that comes through the stage play is going to be a lot more meaningful. That doesn't mean I'm going to write stage plays, but I find from the oral tradition that several things—the presence of the audience, the presence on the stage, the characters and the ability to provide narrators at the sides of the stage or wherever—the ability to use all of those contains an integrity that is required by traditional storytelling: the immediacy of the artist and the intermediary, which is the narrator.

Which urges that idea again that I have also encountered elsewhere that performance may be the better medium for the translation of traditional material than the book. . . . It makes sense.

Yes. Because the formats are really there, the genres are really there.

Do you classify yourself, as a writer, as a realist, a modernist, a postmodern writer? Do you find these terms useful?

[Laughter] I don't even know what those terms are. . . .

I'd probably say a postmodern,[42] although I really dislike that terminology and the categorization as a postmodern. But I couldn't say that I'm a modernist writer. There are a number of reasons, you know, that I think that: probably because of my own concerns, my own philosophical concerns, that's why I would choose that, rather than because of genre or matters of style.

I could change my mind, though.

If a so-called "deconstructive use of language" is regarded as one of the trademarks of the postmodern, that's not necessarily what you do, right? You are not necessarily deconstructing; you are more of a "constructing" writer.

In terms of my philosophy, in terms of deconstructing the accepted literary canon and working from that point, always working from that point, that's why I would place myself there; but I would say in terms of style and the way I use language, I end up pretty modernist and traditional, in that sense.[43]

---

42. *Why?*
Deconstruction seems to be a vehicle toward openness.

43. *We have a hidden problem here that I should have thought of beforehand: the different uses of precisely these terms in U.S. and Canadian writing—quite apart from their basically contested nature.*
Yes, in the sense that it is used for literatures.

There is this baldly phrased question here: The theme or subject of many Indian texts lends itself to treatment in sociological, economic, or narrowly political terms, but the treatment usually does take place in broadly cultural ones. Why?

The background to that is that in talking about some Native texts with students last semester, I suddenly found them being worried that conflict, particularly Native-white conflict, was predominantly being talked about in terms of a conflict of cultures rather than class conflict, economic conflict, things like that. And they then really began asking whether this type of literature does not ultimately hide the material conflict, which was to them in a sense more real, behind the cultural conflict.

How do you want me to comment on that? [Laughter]

Do you find their approach interesting, useful? Do you find the question relevant? I mean, I just phrased it the way I did because I think one could answer them by saying, "Oh, but the cultural side is ultimately the more real one, and the material conflict is not." That would be one possible reaction, but I don't know which one you'd choose.

One could also rephrase the entire question to run something like this: Shouldn't Native literature address the material side of things, the social conflict, the economic conflict, more clearly, more programmatically?

I think probably—you know, I'm not going to construct reasons for any other writers, other than myself![44]—but I think one of the backgrounds to the wellspring of literature and voice has been a voice of resistance and is rooted in an inner voice of resistance. And I don't mean resistance in the sense where we are talking about conflict, but resistance in a sense of resistance to colonialism and resistance to the whole culture clash that is assimilationist in nature (and aggressively assimilationist in nature), and the resistance psychologically to that in terms of the creative voice that arises out of this situation. It has been the main concern, it has been the main reason, the main purpose, to create a voice that basically says: that's not the way it is, *this* is the way it is, this is how it is.

44. *So—is this the kind of basic question (question of basic motivation, basic aim, basic purpose) that the School of Writing does not address, and that perhaps a school of writing should not address—because one is too close to interfering with the sources of creativity here?*

That is always the premise I work from (my postmodern stance again).

But in saying that, what happens is, *it's saying it culturally:* *Culturally,* this is not the way it is; culturally, this is how it is voiced! And voicing that becomes a concern with and a focus on culture rather than a concern and a focus on all of the other social threads that run through, that create that conflict, and that could be focused on in terms of the discourse, whatever it might be, in the text. And I think to some extent some writers are touching on that and beginning to maybe uncover some of those threads, but I find that to a great extent culture is the *vehicle* that takes you to that point: that everything else is colored by it, every conflict is colored through that major concern.

That has been one of the major criticisms from the literary critics in Canada—maybe in the U.S., I'm not sure (I haven't spent a lot of time reading a lot of the major criticism), but it has been so in Canada. It has been one of the major, *major* criticisms from the critics we have and in terms of their approach to looking at the new writings in Native literature. And I think in a sense that's going to be the situation in postcolonial literature for a number of years to come, and in that sense it isn't *post*colonial, and I have said that. In a sense I find that we are immersed in colonial literatures. Even Canadian literatures are colonial literatures; they are not Canadian unless they have been deconstructed to a point in which all Canadian experience (which includes the experience with us as Native peoples) in terms of literary voice is included, and it isn't at this point.

So how can there be a postcolonial literature? There isn't, not from our side or from their side. And so that whole dialogue about the culture and its focus in our writing is very clearly colonial—as colonialist literature—and will be until a number of years have passed and a number of things have been written, out of which emerge the real postcolonial literatures.

So, I mean, that's not justifying it or excusing it, it's saying that that's what happens.

Yes. I also think it has something to do with how notions of race and ethnicity have been more dominant during the last ten years or so than notions of class.

Well, it's probably more difficult to understand the brand of racism if you are not living in this country as a Native indigenous person or as a person of color. This country, like the United States, would have the rest of the world think racism isn't a reality. . . .

Racism is on the increase everywhere. . . .[45]

It's on the increase, and in Canada the special brand of it is that it's systemic, and that systemic racism is not acknowledged as racism; it's never acknowledged as racism, it's never stated as racism. Racism is simply thought about as bigotry.

And it never occurs to the people who make the policies or who make the laws regarding education, regarding religion, regarding even who gets to sanction a marriage—that there is racism there, there is no other word for it. Systemically, *these* people have the right to make those decisions, and systemically, *your* people don't have that right. And "your people" all happen to be— you know, we are not talking about Okanagans, we are talking about a conglomerate group of people who have the same color of skin and the same origin as you do. And they don't dwell on the color of skin, but it just so happens everybody who is dark-skinned and indigenous to this country are in that group.[46]

What do you call that if that's not racism? Okanagans are very, very different than Micmacs, very, very different than Inuit people, culturally, physically, philosophically, everything, yet we are all lumped into one, and policies are made around that lumping. Lumped into one as though we were the same, as though we were no different than each other. That's racism, pure and simple, and that's maybe one of the things that create the resistance; that's the commonality, when we are speaking in terms of the colonialist society and its effect on our literature and our art, that we find ourselves psychologically concerned with those things. Because— in one of my books I mention that—it's like fighting with shadows; you don't really see the face of the enemy because it pretends to be a smiling benevolent face and presents itself that way—"*I* am not racist"—and all the time doing all and everything that says to us,

---

45. *I am not sure that it is clear that I was particularly thinking of Europe here.*

46. *So we have two denials of difference: between the dominant group and "others," so that the latter are forced to obey the rules of the former; and among "others," who are precisely subjected to a wholesale "othering" that makes of a great diversity a single, homogeneous group.*
Yes.

"Yes, you are racist." When you do this and this and this and we resist that, you bring your guns out like they did in Oka. You resist that and you say you are not racist—what *do* you call that? And you are standing there smiling and saying, "This isn't racism; this just happens to be Law and Order, but on *our* terms, and under our definition, not on yours, never on yours."[47]

And so what is it? So we find ourselves subjectively, in our literatures, pursuing those answers and finding and talking to each other of all those questions around that.

In this context, the question of violence: How do you address that question in your works? What would you say? Do your texts advocate an attitude towards violence, a perspective towards violence?

I think they do. I'm not *sure* they do; I'm not the reader on the other end, but I have a philosophy that I would say is best understood in terms of the discourse that I did with Doug Cardinal, in explaining some of that into a philosophy that has a basis in what's sometimes called "pacifism," although I never want it to be confused with pacifism. It resonates pacifism; within that philosophy I feel that ultimately everything can be resolved without conflict because we are given the capacity of our minds and our emotions, and all of the history that we have, all the tools that we have learned, and [the experience of] the things that we have come up against. We have the capacity to resolve without conflict; we have the knowledge to resolve those conflicts.[48]

And so I feel that that's what I pursue in my writing. I pursue that as a common theme in my writing or an attitude in my writing. Conflict is *not* necessary. If we as people, as a variety of people, can rely on our being able to touch each other in certain ways and bring

47. *The play of personal pronouns, with its shifting inclusion and exclusion of me, the non-Indian interlocutor, is here indicative of the stresses of the political situation addressed.*

I was referring to the "lumping together" of Canada's political system of racism which constructs an "us" and "them."

48. *Two notions of conflict: there is conflict, but we can resolve it without creating more conflict?*

This is my attitude toward violence addressed within my text: I am human, I have been equipped to preserve my life and my family's lives—I must, no question—but I will be more successful at that *if I resolve* conflict rather than engage in conflict, so resistance to *domination* is *constant* in an adversarial milieu.

understanding to each other in certain ways, connecting with minds and hearts, we can resolve any things which may occur as possible conflicts between us.

However, conflict in terms of violence *is* necessary—and anything else as self-defense is important. Self-defense—whether you want to think about it in that way or not, if your survival depends on it, without thinking you will react violently. That's an imperative that we're given to live, and that's an imperative that we share with every other life form on this earth. That's not something that we can recode or change or whatever. Violence *is* necessary for self-defense and self-preservation, and it is justifiable for that. That doesn't mean that violence should be used, that violence is necessary to be used, when other means to resolve conflict are there. *All* should be used before violence, because violence in the end defeats the purpose. . . .

Why?

. . . Violence in the end defeats life.

What is the source of evil?

[Laughter]

It's a question that seems to come automatically afterwards.

I think probably lack of knowledge. I think probably ignorance may be the best definition I would have.

You are an Enlightenment person?

I guess.

I feel very deeply that if there is knowledge and there is understanding and clarity, no evil is possible, because the choices that must be made must be made with clarity, and if they are hard choices, they are inherently not evil because they *have* to be made, whether it's for the good of the people or for the preservation of the individual. Evil is not a question in that.

This is going to be one of the points where you differ most from the two other authors—it's interesting. It may have something to do with the gender question, too.

Possibly.

[Laughter]

Since I dragged the gender question in just now: Indian writing tries to construct a sense of difference. Feminist writing tries to do the same. Now the interesting thing is that in feminist writing you get far more blueprints for a concrete future. You get utopias, you get science fiction writing that tries to construct utopias etc. You don't seem to be getting that sort of thing too much in Indian writing—why not?

That's a good question, and I think the question has to do with why the focus is on cultural writing, on writing about culture.

There seems to have been a transition in perspective in literatures that have emerged from various Indian writers, Native writers. In the past, I would say, thirty years or something like that, there's been a transition. And if you follow a few, or if you were to list all the writers, and if you were to list their focus and perspectives and the themes that are running through their writing, one of the things that becomes apparent is the focus on contemporary change and contemporary analysis of society, and on how Native peoples traditionally or in a contemporary context revolve around their origin, their tradition, their values, and then how they survive within that.

Simple survival within that seems to be the main focus, the main concern; it's in surviving *today*—how did we do it yesterday, and how do we do it today—because surviving today is extremely critical. Because they are *not* surviving. Many, many of our people are not surviving. And the problem of the wellness of our people in our communities at this point is evident; it's a daily concern. The people and characters of our stories are real in the sense that everyday there's suicide, everyday there is violence in which wives get beaten up and beaten to death, or young teenagers kill themselves driving too fast on the road, or fighting with each other, whatever. Those are real people who people our stories, and our concern with that is a concern of the now, right today, of the present rather than of the future; and I think that one of the reasons that it occurs that way is an attempt to bring forward some of the knowledge of the past and reinterpret that into the present to make the present more understandable, and therefore our chances for survival in terms of. . .

Make it viable. . . .

Yes, make it viable. For today's survival writing becomes more useful than other means.

And in that sense the concern has been almost totally that. It's almost like saying, "How can I plan for ten years from now when I'm just planning today? Where should I get the bread to feed my family? You know, you can't plan for ten years from now if that's what your immediate concern is: just to feed your family. So, in the same sense, the analogy in our writing is how we are going to—in terms of our communities—say the things and write the things that are necessary to keep our families and communities going in an everyday sense, in a daily sense, in the present—let alone thinking about ten years from now.

How do we make sense of today, you know?

Yet out there, in that other room there, there was a blueprint for a new community center.

Yes.

So in other media and for things like that there is planning ahead for the next decade. But literature is at least momentarily focused on survival?

I haven't seen anything, unless you have.

No, I haven't.

I haven't seen any futuristic writing.

We are publishing—I think Theytus this year is publishing—in the science fiction genre for the first time, a Native writer; and that should be an interesting thing for critics to look at and read. I found the text of that most interesting, and I want to see more of that kind of writing; I am excited about more of that. I don't mean science fiction as a genre, but writing about the future.

I think that is a good point to stop. Let's stop with the future.[49]

49. *One might speculate on why the literature may find it more difficult to address that question of (the possibility of) a future. Is this hard-nosed realism or a failure of nerve? Or has literature as a whole, and as an institution (with some exceptions), lost the knack of addressing the future?*

It has been my observation that perhaps it has overall, and perhaps for the same reasons. This is interesting in light of the shifting social constructs which are creating massive rapid change affecting all peoples in their immediate lives.